# ZAC EFRON

# ZAC EFRON

## A-Z

ALEX KINCAID

JB

JOHN BLAKE

Published by John Blake Publishing Ltd,
3 Bramber Court, 2 Bramber Road,
London W14 9PB, England

www.johnblakepublishing.co.uk

First published in paperback in 2010

ISBN: 978 1 84358 303 5

British Library Cataloguing-in-Publication Data:

A catalogue record for this book is available from the British Library.

Design by www.envydesign.co.uk

Printed in Great Britain by CPI Bookmarque, Croydon, CR0 4TD

1 3 5 7 9 10 8 6 4 2

Papers used by John Blake Publishing are natural, recyclable products made from
wood grown in sustainable forests. The manufacturing processes conform to the
environmental regulations of the country of origin.

# Introduction

The *Zac Efron A–Z* is a complete and up-to-date guide to all things Zac.

Zachary David Alexander Efron seemed to burst onto the scene as a fully-fledged star when he wowed the world in *High School Musical* – but in reality, the apparent 'overnight success' had taken years of dedicated work.

Zac is not the sort of star who courts the limelight or tells the world what he's thinking. He's quite a private person; modest and down to earth. This book looks at Zac's roles in film and TV, but also covers his family, his friends, and what he thinks about acting and being famous – everything that has made him the person he is.

The A–Z format means that you can read it from start to finish, or pick it up to dip into – whatever suits you!

# A is for...

## Accidents

In many ways, Zac is a very sensible and down to earth guy – but from time to time he does take risks or let his mind wander, and this appears to make him a little bit accident prone. He told the *Mirror* newspaper that one of his more embarrassing accidents occurred when he was younger and he tried to impress a girl at school by doing a back flip off the swings. He'd managed to perform this particular stunt many times before, but when it came to the crunch, it went badly wrong. Zac ended up flat on his back on the ground, winded… while the girl in question burst out laughing and walked off. Ooops!

While Zac was filming the song 'What Time is It?' for *High School Musical 2* a desk fell on his foot, causing a bad swelling. And he used to be really keen on skateboarding, but was told to give up after a bad crash. 'I slammed my back, shoulders and head into the bottom of a half-pipe,' he confessed. Zac started skateboarding as a child and loves it. He even has a collection of skateboards – so who knows if he will manage to give up, even with the risk of hurting himself again!

# Acting

Zac didn't come from a typical show business family, and a career in acting wasn't always his ambition. 'I wouldn't say this was my dream,' he once said in an interview. 'I didn't have any plans or aspirations to be an actor. It was always my hobby – it was always my extra-curricular and what I did for fun outside of school. Then it started to pay for college and it

# ALEX KINCAID

ZAC'S BIG ON-SCREEN BREAK CAME AFTER HE LANDED THE ROLE OF TROY IN *HIGH SCHOOL MUSICAL*.

5

became slightly more serious, and then I discovered that this would probably be a fun direction to head in life.'

It may have started out as fun, but Zac also takes his acting pretty seriously. Despite the dozens of offers he has had to reprise his success in teen dramas and musicals, he doesn't want to stagnate and do the same thing over and over again. Instead, he tries to choose roles that continue to challenge him and he wants each part he plays to give him something new to learn. He is proud of the fact that he's willing to keep learning, and he absolutely refuses to cut any corners. 'For any movie, if there's a skill set that's required, whether it's riding horses, basketball, golf, sports, athletics, anything like that, I take pride in the fact that I can learn those things for a role,' he says. This commitment and attention to detail are also things that are valued by the directors Zac has worked with.

Zac is clearly very happy with his career so far, and frequently talks about how lucky he feels to have landed great roles, but he admits that he sometimes finds it frustrating to have so much attention on him as a so-called 'teen idol' rather than on his acting. He feels that the adoration he's received, and especially the focus that is so often placed on his undoubted good looks, has caused its fair share of problems. 'It's such a fine line between being famous for who you are personally and for your films. And I've been on the wrong side of it my whole career. I don't want to be famous for my personality. If anything, I keep that under wraps.'

But these problems aside, Zac clearly loves what he does – he wouldn't stay in the business otherwise. And he has this advice for anyone who is considering following in his footsteps: 'Do it because you love doing it. Don't do anything just to be famous. It would really suck if you had the fame without the love for what you do,' he says.

# Advice

Lots of Zac's friends and co-stars have said that he is a good person to go to when they need some advice. Ashley Tisdale, one of his friends from his time on *High School Musical*, says that she frequently rings him up when she needs a guy's take on something, and his *17 Again* co-star, Sterling Knight, said that Zac gave him some really good advice on his career. Perhaps because Zac has done a lot of projects set in schools (*High School Musical*, *17 Again*, *Hairspray*) he is often

asked about his own schooldays and if he has any advice for teenagers based on his experiences.

Zac is very sympathetic to kids who don't have a great time at school – lots of people are surprised to find that he wasn't a popular Troy Bolton-type figure at his own high school. He worked hard, wasn't part of the super-cool set and was scared to talk to girls! He says that the key thing he thinks that teenagers should try to do is to keep pushing the boundaries and find out what they really want from their lives. When he was making the *High School Musical* films, Zac said that his advice was: 'Try and do something that scares you every day. It's the only way you can test how far you can really go; whether it's going out and auditioning for the play or trying out for the basketball team, you have to explore your boundaries and see where you really want to go, and the only way you can do that is to break out of your shell.'

This was pretty wise advice from someone who was, at the time, barely out of school himself! And his other key message is not to plan too much, and not to dwell on things you can't change. 'Live in the moment, live for right now. Don't worry about the past.'

OPPOSITE: ZAC'S *17 AGAIN* CO-STAR STERLING KNIGHT.

# Ambition

Nearly every time Zac is interviewed, the interviewer describes him as down to earth, normal or modest – but despite this, he is a very driven person who hates to be idle. 'Since I was young, I've always believed in challenging myself. I've been very proactive from a very young age. I don't like to be stagnant.' This means that sometimes he struggles with a career as an actor – not because of the job, but because sometimes there are times when he's expected to take a break! 'The hardest time for me is in-between filming, because I sometimes feel I'm not doing anything,' he says.

This relentless ambition is now channelled into his acting – but it's not stardom he's after. He enjoys the fruits of his success but has not been seduced by the trappings of fame – that isn't what motivates him. 'It's not my ambition to be famous. I want to be the best actor I can possibly be,' he insists. And this ambition is likely to keep him completely focused. Zac's father David has seen his son develop a very determined streak over the years. 'When Zac really wants something,' he told a magazine, 'he can be ruthless in his pursuit.'

ZAC IS NOW ONE OF
THE HOTTEST ACTORS
IN HOLLYWOOD

# Arroyo Grande

Zac was born in San Luis Obispo, a Californian town halfway between San Francisco and Los Angeles, and he grew up in nearby Arroyo Grande. Arroyo Grande is a small town with a very tight-knit community – fewer than 5,000 families live there – and Zac attributes his famously down to earth attitude to his non-showbiz upbringing and the surroundings of his home town. The coastal town has pretty tree-lined streets, lots of small, family-run shops, and hosts a Strawberry Festival every spring. Zac always stresses in interviews how normal his childhood was – how he wasn't the cool kid at school, how he played with his friends in fields filled with cows, which they would try to shoot with slingshots. We can appreciate the point he's making, even if we might feel a bit sorry for the cows!

His mum, Starla, agrees with Zac on this, and told an interviewer: 'Zac was raised very grounded. He was busy here in town doing plays and all that. He's had the same friends all his life, and he didn't really get into the Hollywood scene. Thank heaven for that. He's still Zac. That's from growing up here.'

# Ashley Tisdale

Ashley played the role of the popular but scheming and self-obsessed Sharpay Evans in the *High School Musical* films. She wasn't considered for the part at first, because the Disney Channel producers thought she had too much of a 'good girl' image! But she certainly found a way to convey the cattiness she needed to make the part her own.

Like the rest of the *High School Musical* cast, Ashley is good friends with Zac. They regularly go to dinner and concerts together, and sometimes even work out together at the gym. He has often talked about her as being a close friend, describing her as 'one of the nicest girls I've ever met,' and Ashley is happy to talk about how well they get along. She says, 'He's so funny, and you can just chill and hang out with him. We met years ago through a mutual friend, so we were friends for a long time before *High School Musical*.' It sounds as though Zac must give Ashley some advice on her love life from time to time, because she's also said that she likes having someone who will be completely honest with her and someone 'who can give you a guy's opinion. And if I have a problem, I know I can call him whenever.'

Zac's *High School Musical* co-star, Ashley Tisdale

Being such good friends with Zac can cause problems, though. When Zac and Ashley had to kiss when they appeared together in *Suite Life*, Ashley said that she found it very odd. This may be unbelievable to many of Zac's fans, but she described having to kiss our favourite star as 'disgusting!': 'It was! He's my best friend and so he's like my brother. I've never been attracted to him because he looked like he was 12 when I met him; so when I had to kiss him in the episode I'm like, first of all it's my best friend's boyfriend and it's awkward enough. But it's like kissing your brother almost...' They must have got over the initial awkwardness, because Ashley added that 'he made it really fun and comfortable' in the end.

# Auditioning

Zac might be offered his pick of starring roles these days, but acting jobs haven't always come as easily to him as they do now. At the start of his career, he had to work hard for his breaks, and his mother used to take him to auditions three days a week. 'For every role that I have done on TV and movies, I've auditioned for 30 or 40,' he says.

It was Zac's dad who took him to his first audition for a musical, and although Zac wasn't very keen on the idea at first, he did well and got the part. 'Little did I know my dad had just showed me the coolest thing on earth at the time. He opened so many doors for me. I started auditioning for every single play that was in our area. Luckily, I booked some of the roles and started doing very well.'

After success in musical theatre, he had a rocky start in auditions for TV. His first TV audition was for a part in Peter Pan – and Zac had just finished a run in the stage show, so he went into the audition feeling very confident! 'On stage, you speak to the back of the room and you project and Peter Pan is very animated and jumping off things and going crazy – so that's what I did. This woman interrupted me and goes, "You've never done this before, have you?" and I said, "No" and she said "OK, you can go," and that was the worst audition ever, ever in my life.' Fortunately, things have got a lot better since then!

Even when you hit the big time, it isn't all plain sailing. Even the biggest stars will still have disappointments, shortlists that they don't make, auditions that don't go well, projects that don't work out or that fall through. Zac is realistic in his approach to every audition and with every possibility

A COOL LOOKING
MR EFRON ARRIVES
AT YET ANOTHER
FILM PREMIÈRE.

that comes up for a part. He knows what he wants, and does what he can to get it – but if things go wrong, he doesn't dwell on it. 'You have to do your best every time. But after each audition, you have to forget about it,' he says. 'You always have to be looking forward and not looking back.' This attitude – doing his best but not beating himself up if it doesn't work out – is part of the down to earth approach that Zac is noted for.

# Awards

For an actor who is only 22 years old, and who has appeared in a relatively small number of films, Zac has gathered an impressive collection of awards – and has been nominated for many more.

Zac has been a favourite at the Teen Choice Awards since 2006 – not surprising given his starting out in *High School Musical* – and has won awards for both his acting and his looks. In 2009 he won two acting awards: the 'Choice Movie Actor: Comedy' award for *17 Again* and the 'Choice Movie Actor: Music/Dance' award for *High School Musical 3*.

On *Hairspray*, Zac was part of an 'ensemble' cast –

Zac at the Teen Choice Awards in 2007.

one with lots of lead characters who all take big roles, but no single 'star'. The cast were nominated for the Screen Actors Guild award in 2008, but unfortunately, they weren't lucky on the night. They did, however, take away the ensemble awards at both the Palm Springs Film Festival and the Hollywood Film Festival. As well as sharing the honours with the rest of the cast, Zac was singled out for an award of his own for *Hairspray* when he won the Young Hollywood Award as 'One to Watch'.

More recently, our favourite actor has been a staple at the MTV Movie Awards – he won the award for Best Male Performance in 2009 for *High School Musical*, and said that winning was 'crazy. It's the last thing you expect.' That success was followed by a nomination (again for the Best Male Performance award) for *17 Again*. And in June 2010, he was honoured with a 'Shining Star Award' at the Maui Film Festival. The festival's organisers say that this award is designed to honour a film actor who is 'still in the ascendance of their career – with many magnetic performances both behind and ahead of them – whose very presence on screen guarantees as much light as heat.' All of this sounds like quite a tall order, but when the award was presented, Zac was hailed as 'an actor with abundant talent, an extraordinary career behind him and an even more brilliant one ahead of him, an exemplary shining star.' Wow! Zac said that the award was a great honour, and that he hoped to live up to the trust that had been put in him.

# B is for...

## Best friends

Zac is clearly someone who makes friends easily, and there are a lot of people who describe him as their best friend, and just as many whom he calls his best friend. He puts a lot of effort into keeping in touch with the people close to him – some months he sends more than 1,500 texts to his friends! He has mentioned his seven closest friends from his childhood: Taylor, Shane, Conner, Chris, Bubba, Bryce, and Jorn. He says, 'I've hung out with them all the way from diapers to this day.' One of the seven, Chris, expands on this: 'I have known Zac since elementary school. He's a great guy and has stayed down to earth and genuine, despite his international success. He always has and always will be a great

Zac enjoys loads of different types of activities in his spare time, including surfing and even bungee jumping!

friend.' Chris has no doubts that Zac will continue to be the mate he has always been. 'Money wasn't his reason for going into acting. Zac is just so passionate about it. That's why I know being famous won't change him.'

Zac appreciates having friends who aren't in the same line of work as him, because they give him a chance to be 'normal' and escape the pressures of his career. Also, his friends have all known him so long that they have seen the gradual process Zac has gone through to get to where he is, so they don't feel at all intimidated by his success. 'I'm lucky enough to have friends that are so far removed from the industry that they do not care,' says Zac. 'I come home and it's a reality check'. 'Keeping it real' is obviously something that he finds very important, and his friends are a key part of that. His old mates are very proud of Zac's success, but they're not above passing on a bit of frank criticism if they think it's needed. Zac isn't bothered by this at all. He trusts their opinions and values that part of his friendships with them. 'The best advice they give me is to critique my work,' he says

He has also said that his old friends are a big part of his comfort factor, and relishes the fact that he knows he can rely on them. 'I never had to look for friends because I always knew I had my buddies back home.' But despite this feeling of security in his old friendships, he has gone on to form real and lasting friendships with some of his co-stars from his various film and TV projects. He has talked a lot about the close friendships he formed with his co-stars in the *High School Musical* films, and after filming *Hairspray*, he described Brittany Snow and Nikki Blonsky as his new best friends. Claire Danes wrote an article about him for *Time* magazine, after they had worked together on *Me and Orson Welles*, in which her genuine affection for him comes across very clearly. And then, of course, there's Vanessa. When Zac was asked if he'd like to do another project with her, he said, 'Sure, I hope so. It's always great getting to work with your best friend.' That's what comes of him being so likeable and so willing to devote time to maintaining his friendships – so many of Zac's friends say how supportive he is that it's no surprise that he has so many friends.

## Body

Zac got the honour of being named as having the hottest body of 2010 by *People* magazine. They produced a special edition featuring the '50 best bodies in Hollywood' and our favourite star appeared on the cover in a shot taken on the beach in Hawaii. He says he owes his great conditioning to his hour-long workouts in the gym where he does weights to improve his muscle tone as well as cardiovascular exercise to keep fit. Whatever the details of his exercise routine, it certainly seems to be working...

# Books

Zac says that English was his favourite subject at school, and he still really enjoys reading. He reads to prepare for his roles and also for pleasure. He says that he enjoys reading because he thinks books can convey a story better: 'In the first few pages of a book, you can find 10 times as much detail as in a movie or a TV show.'

Zac has fairly eclectic tastes in reading material. He's a big fan of graphic novels and comics, and has been since he was small (he says he would wait avidly for new Spider-man comics when he was six years old!). He has said that his favourite books include

ZAC ARRIVES AT
LAX AIRPORT, AFTER
A FLIGHT FROM NEW
YORK CITY.

Daniel Defoe's *Robinson Crusoe* and Ben Mezrich's *Busting Vegas,* which is about a group of students who used their mathematics skills to win at blackjack in Las Vegas casinos.

# Brittany Snow

Brittany played the scheming, gossipy Amber von Tussel in *Hairspray*. At the start of the movie, Amber is the girlfriend of Zac's character, Link Larkin, but she gradually puts him off with her bitchy tactics. Despite their on-screen falling out, Zac and Brittany got on very well off-screen – leading to the inevitable rumours that they were dating. This may not have been helped by Brittany being rather vocal about how attractive Zac is. 'I would have to say Zac is one of the hottest guys I've worked with,' she gushed to journalists, while Zac described his co-star as one of his best friends.

Despite all the gossip, the pair really *were* just good friends. 'Zac is one of the most genuine, sweetest people that I've met, and he deserves every good thing that comes to him,' Brittany said. Brittany is yet another of Zac's friends and co-stars who is at pains

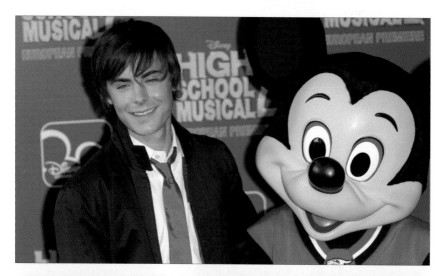

*Above*: A youthful looking Zac at the première of *High School Musical 2* alongside a very special guest.

*Below*: Our favourite actor poses for the cameras at the première of *17 Again*.

*Above*: Vanessa Hudgens, Zac, Ashley Tisdale and Corbin Bleu at the London première of *High School Musical 3*.

*Left*: Vanessa and Zac are reported to have been dating since the first *High School Musical* film.

Zac at the Teen Choice
Awards in 2009.

*Above*: Zac and the *Hairspray* cast perform for television in 2007.

*Below*: Swarmed by his adoring fans, Zac takes to the surf on Bondi Beach, Australia.

Our favourite actor poses for pictures outside a television studio.

Zac waves to the crowd alongside Vanessa at the *High School Musical* press conference in 2007.

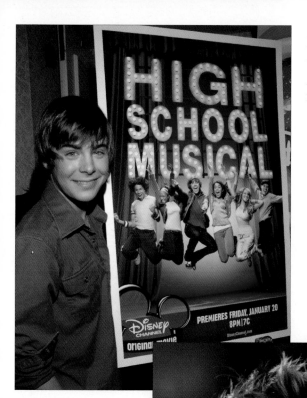

*Left*: Zac poses next to the poster of his breakthrough film *High School Musical* in 2005.

*Right*: Five years after his star turn as Troy in *High School Musical*, Zac is now one of the hottest actors in Hollywood.

Zac at the L.A. prèmiere of *Charlie St. Cloud.*

to make clear how down to earth and normal he is. 'He really is just a normal, sweet, charismatic guy, and he's very special.' Despite their busy lifestyles, this is a friendship that has lasted the time since they worked together. Zac and Vanessa made it to Brittany's birthday party, and earlier this year they had a double lunch date with Brittany and her boyfriend Ryan Rottman.

# Bungee jumping

Zac has always been into outdoors activity and it sounds like he's a bit of a thrill seeker – he has said that he really wants to go skydiving. Eeek! So, when he had the chance to have a go at bungee jumping (while in Canada filming *Charlie St. Cloud*), he threw caution to the wind and had a go. Not just once, but twice!

He told TV host David Letterman that some of the cast and crew had what he called 'this brilliant idea to wake up in the morning and go bungee jumping.' And so he found himself throwing himself off a bridge outside Vancouver, a drop of about 275 feet towards a river. Not content with just doing the jump, Zac apparently did a back-flip on the way off.

He did admit that bungee jumping while you're making a film isn't the wisest thing to do, not least because 'you've signed a lot of contracts saying you won't do that stuff.' The production company were apparently quite upset when they found out, because there was a risk that Zac could have got hurt. They were, Zac said, 'almost as upset as my dad. He was like "What were you thinking?!"' But Zac said he'd considered the risks and it seemed that it was a risk worth taking. 'C'mon – How often is the rope gonna snap?' he said.

# Burr Steers

Zac has worked with director Burr Steers on two films, *17 Again* and the new movie *Charlie St. Cloud*, which is due out in 2010. Zac revealed that when they worked on *17 Again*, he didn't get on brilliantly with Burr at first, until he realised that his prickly persona was actually part of his direction technique. 'He messed with my head a little bit,' Zac says of Steers. He says that there were some scenes in the film where he had to be annoyed, so Burr would be horrible to him: 'to make me a little

Burr Steers with his wife at the *Charlie St. Cloud* première.

bit on edge. I had no idea what he was doing until after the movie was over.' No wonder Zac didn't like Burr very much! 'But it turns out he's incredibly smart,' Zac continued. 'He doesn't just give you what you want to hear and tell you that you're doing a great job. It's a different kind of love and support.' So, once these teething problems were in the past, Zac was keen to work with Burr again, and was excited to sign up to play the lead in *Charlie St. Cloud*. We'll all be able to see the results when the film is released in October 2010.

# C is for...

## Cars

Zac describes cars as his only extravagance – although even when he's being extravagant, he's still very sensible. 'I don't have a fleet of cars,' he told the *Daily Mail*. 'It's smarter to live below your means. Whatever you can afford, go two pegs down and you're safe.' So, no doing the film star thing and splashing the cash on a garage full of cars, then? One of his more recent purchases is a black Audi S6, but he also enjoys restoring vintage cars, a pastime he shares with his engineer father and his grandfather. 'I wouldn't say I'm great, but I get a lot of guidance,' he says. 'I got the bug from my dad. He rebuilt his first eight cars. My grandfather loves working on cars, too.'

But what does he keep in his car? Apparently, he always makes sure he keeps some film memorabilia in the boot, because he finds that it can come in useful for securing favours. He said he first learned of the ruse when he pulled into a car park to avoid photographers. 'The guy at the gate was like, "What

OUR FAVOURITE ACTOR ENJOYS DRIVING BETWEEN AUDITIONS AND FILM SHOOTS.

are you going to do for me?" I said, "What do you want me to do?" He's like, "I got kids." And I was like, "Well, I got a poster in the trunk!'" Sneaky!

# Charlie St. Cloud

Zac's latest film is due out in the UK in October 2010. It has been described as a fantasy romance and is based on a novel by Ben Sherwood called *The Death and Life of Charlie St. Cloud*. This was the second film that Zac had worked on with director Burr Steers, and after their partnership in *17 Again*, Zac was keen to sign up to the project, which also stars Ray Liotta and Kim Basinger.

Zac stars as the Charlie St. Cloud of the title, who survives a car accident in which his much loved younger brother, Sam, is killed. Before the accident, Charlie had promised to practise baseball with Sam every day until he left for college. At the funeral, Charlie is overcome with grief and he sees Sam's ghost, who reminds him of the promise he made to him. Charlie takes a job as the caretaker of the cemetery where Sam is buried, and continues to develop his special bond with his little brother.

But then things get complicated, as they invariably do when romance enters the mix. Charlie meets a girl, Tess (played by Amanda Crew), and gradually develops strong feelings for her. As Tess and Charlie become closer, Charlie feels torn – he can't keep his promise to Sam and find happiness with his new love. So, which will he choose? We'll be watching in October to find out, and judging by the trailer, which you can see online, there won't be a dry eye in the cinemas, so stock up on tissues!

Zac says that he's really excited about his fans seeing the movie, because it's so different from anything he's done before – there's an unusual storyline and it has a very different emotional feel to it. He was drawn to the story because it's about a relationship between brothers – and he has a strong relationship with his younger brother Dylan. 'Growing up it was me and him against the world,' says Zac, 'so I really connected with the material.' The new emotional range was the challenge for Zac – he found making the film really intense. 'There were a lot of moments that became real for me and that was a new challenge,' he admitted in an interview at the Maui Film Festival.

OPPOSITE: ZAC AT THE LA PREMIÈRE OF *CHARLIE ST. CLOUD*

# Choosing roles

When it comes to thinking about the sort of projects he'd like to work on in the future, Zac is definitely keeping an open mind. 'I would love to try everything from horror to action to straight comedy – there is so much in this business that you can do,' he says.

Continuing his recent trend of choosing something new each time he makes a film, Zac is keen not to rule anything out. He's aware that if he's going to build on his success he will need to take the right roles at the right times, which might mean waiting for the chance to have a go at some of the films he really wants.

He loves the idea of action films, but says that taking a fully-fledged action role too soon would be a 'kiss of death' – both to the movie and to his career. 'There's got to be a real role that I can bring something unique and specific to, a way for me to do it believably. Until then, I think it would just come across as weird,' he says, candidly. He loves films like *Pulp Fiction* – anything with a good character and a good gritty story – but he says he wants to make some films which will build up the respect for his acting that would be necessary for those kinds of roles. Zac has

Zac is a massive fan of all the Bond films and his favourite 007 is Sean Connery.

also got his eye on a role in a future James Bond film, and describes himself as a huge Bond fan – but he has no ambition to take on the role of 007. Instead, he wants to play the villain. He says 'I'd love to be a Bond baddie. I've seen pretty much every Bond film. Sean Connery is my favourite Bond.'

But Zac says that he was very struck by someone saying that 'you need to earn the right to hold a gun' – meaning that you need to get the right image and the right level of professional respect before it will work – and he doesn't think he's there yet. 'Can you imagine me running around with a gun in a film?' he asked. 'I noticed the second I started that the things you want to be involved with are always just out of reach. Most parts you'd want, people won't really consider you for, because you have to earn that respect.' Zac is also aware that he needs to take the right jobs to build his profile if he wants to get the chance to work with the directors he most admires. 'Most of the directors I'd want to work with don't even know who I am,' he admits, referring to his 'teen idol' image. 'Their daughters might.'

So, it looks like Zac is content to play the long game, choose his roles carefully, watch and wait – and his fans have all the more reason to follow his career with interest.

# Christian McKay

Christian McKay was Zac's co-star in *Me and Orson Welles* and judging from the interviews he gave at the time, he clearly enjoyed working with our favourite star. The British actor, who was widely acclaimed for his unnervingly accurate portrayal of iconic American director Orson Welles, heaped praise on Zac when he was interviewed at the London première of the film. 'Zac is a wonderful actor, it was wonderful to work with him,' he said. Christian is an experienced stage actor, but this was his first film role. Referring to his character's famously bossy directional style, he joked, 'It was a pleasure to shout at him and boss him around. I had a whale of a time!'

Christian's admiration for Zac's talent was definitely reciprocated. Zac described Christian as 'such a star' and said that he was great to work with. Like the critics, he was totally astonished by McKay's performance as Orson Welles, saying, 'When he read his lines for the first time as Orson [on the first day of rehearsals], I was shocked. I was floored.'

Christian also warned Hollywood not to underestimate Zac or his abilities, saying, 'He's 22 and people want to put him in a pigeonhole because of the

CHRISTIAN MCKAY STARRED ALONGSIDE ZAC IN THE HIT FILM,
*ME AND ORSON WELLES.*

success of his earlier films. But the world's his oyster, he can do anything.' He added that he was looking forward to seeing the films Zac makes in the future – and it's safe to say that he's probably not alone in that.

# Cinema

Zac doesn't just make films for a living – he also enjoys watching them in his spare time. He says that he makes a real effort to see as many films as he can in the cinema, rather than relying on DVD at home. He doesn't seem to have a favourite genre, as he's appreciated comedies, action films and science fiction – recently he revealed that he had seen James Cameron's *Avatar* four times. Given Zac's start in musicals, it's not surprising that he has his favourite musical films, namely *Grease* and *Singing in the Rain*. Zac says he has seen *Singing in the Rain* dozens of times, and Gene Kelly is one of his idols.

Part of the appeal of going to the movie theatre is, apparently, not just what's showing on the big screen: Zac describes going to the movies as his preferred option for a date. When asked what the perfect date movie would be, Zac played the gentleman and said, 'Whatever she wants to see.' But then he undermined

ONE OF ZAC'S ALL-TIME FAVOURITE MUSICAL FILMS IS *GREASE*, STARRING
JOHN TRAVOLTA AND OLIVIA NEWTON-JOHN.

the chivalrous image by saying that the cinema was perfect for dates because 'it's dark and everyone's facing the one direction'!

# Claire Danes

Zac was feeling pretty out of his comfort zone when he took on the role of Richard in 1930s period drama *Me and Orson Welles*, and part of that was the worry of living up to working with Claire Danes. He found the prospect quite intimidating. 'I needed to be a worthy love interest in the film and I didn't know that I had any of the qualities necessary to woo a girl like her,' said Zac, with his usual modesty. Even after they had made the film together, he still described women like Claire as being 'out of his league.'

Claire would probably say that he shouldn't be so sure about that. She wrote an entry for Zac in the influential *Time* magazine, in which she not only paid tribute to his abilities as an actor, but also talked about how attractive he is. 'Zac is not only an actor but also a musician, a bona fide song-and-dance man. We ladies are defenceless against such a combination,' she wrote, adding that she was sure

*ME AND ORSON WELLES* CO-STAR CLAIRE DANES THINKS ZAC WILL MAKE LADIES SWOON FOR MANY YEARS TO COME!

that Zac would 'make us swoon for many years to come.' But what's really clear from the article is how much she admired Zac's talent as an actor. She says he's capable of great subtlety in his performance, and works with humility and enthusiasm, and the result, she says, is 'breathtaking'.

# Clothes

Zac's personal style has changed a lot during his time in the public eye. Back in the early days, during and just after the filming of *High School Musical*, he favoured a casual look – lots of jeans and t-shirts – and when he was asked about his favourite footwear, he went for sandals. But he has decided to sharpen up his style quite a lot lately, and has developed a liking for suits. He bought just one to start with, but now he has what he calls 'a collection' although he hasn't admitted how many that is! He also says that most of his personal style is built around accessories – 'it's all about accessories,' he laughed during a recent interview.

Does he follow fashion? Well, yes he does, but only up to a point. He doesn't aspire to be a fashion trendsetter, but he does want to look good. 'I do try and look my best when I'm out and representing my

ZAC LIKES TO KEEP IT
CASUAL WHEN TRAVELLING
BETWEEN FILM SETS.

movies,' he says. As for high fashion, he does pay attention to what's going on, even if he doesn't wear too much of it himself: 'I notice fashion on other people, I always enjoy it when people try and look their best.'

He's also got the odd little secret hidden in his wardrobe – because he likes to pinch a 'souvenir' from the movies he works on. 'Always steal some of your wardrobe. You never know when you might need it,' he says, cheekily. Apparently, this is not an uncommon habit among actors, and on the last day of filming, the costume people are ready and waiting to step in and avert the damage. 'On the last day, they always try to get you out of your trailer really quick so nothing's missing!' Who knew that the clean-living Mr Efron would be involved in such a naughty tradition?

# Corbin Bleu

Corbin played Chad Danforth in the *High School Musical* films. Chad is the best friend of Zac's character, Troy Bolton, and the two soon developed an off-screen friendship that mirrored their on-

screen one. Zac and Corbin still like to hang out with each other and even attended the 2006 World Cup together in Germany. Corbin really enjoyed making the movies, and said of his fellow cast members: 'We've shared so many once-in-a-lifetime experiences together that nobody else will understand, so it's a unique relationship. You know how you relate to somebody if you go through something special together? It's exactly like that. You just connect. We've got chemistry both on screen and off screen – and I'm definitely going to stay in touch with them.' Zac has talked about how he learned some key basketball skills from Corbin to prepare for his role in *High School Musical*. 'I could not spin a ball on my finger for years when I was growing up. I always thought it was cool,' he says. 'Corbin could do it on *High School Musical* and then I couldn't, so…I had to do it. So now Corbin and I do it all day and we just pass balls back and forth to each other.' Spinning a ball on his finger is something that Zac is frequently asked to do during interviews – and he's always willing to oblige, and usually credits Corbin for teaching him!

OPPOSITE: CORBIN AND ZAC AT THE PREMIÈRE OF *HIGH SCHOOL MUSICAL 2*.

# Courtney Cox-Arquette

Courteney Cox-Arquette thinks Zac would be a very good catch for a 'cougar'. And we're not talking about the big cat here. The *Friends* actress has a starring role in the drama *Cougar Town*, playing a woman who likes to date much younger men. Like Leslie Mann, his co-star in *17 Again,* who said that she had to resist the temptation to come over all 'lady cougar' round Zac, Courtney thinks that Zac would be a prime target for real-life cougars . 'Zac Efron would be perfect, but he probably has too much confidence to be real prey for a cougar. You know you're a cougar when you're attracted to your son's friends,' said the 45-year-old actress, who isn't really a *proper* cougar – her husband is only seven years younger than she is!

# Criticism

Hard as it might be for some of his fans to believe, not everyone appreciates our favourite actor, and Zac has got used to handling the criticism that comes his way. When it's from people whose opinion he values,

*FRIENDS* STAR COURTNEY COX-ARQUETTE.

he welcomes it, and when he can, he tries to learn from it. But there are times when he decides it's best to just try to avoid the negativity. 'I can't even go on IMDB because I know that so much of it would be negative,' he says. 'It's just depressing.'

But he also knows not to take the criticism too seriously. He heard about an 'I Hate Zac Efron' club at his cousin's school and didn't take that to heart at all. 'I laughed hysterically when I heard that. I laughed because if there are people out there devoted enough to make a club that hates me, I've gotta be doing something right.' Zac's many fans would all agree that yes, he's definitely doing something right!

# Crushes

Of course, there are thousands of girls all over the world who would happily admit that they have a massive crush on Zac, but our favourite actor is no stranger to having crushes himself. He says that he had his first crush in primary school, and he's still good friends with the girl in question. When he was growing up, he had a crush on model and actress Tyra Banks and had a poster of her, not on his wall, but on

ZAC ADMITS THAT HE ONCE HAD A PICTURE OF TYRA BANKS ON HIS BEDROOM CEILING!

his ceiling. 'And I had a bunk bed,' he told *Seventeen* magazine, 'so she was, like, *really* close.' More recently (apart from Vanessa, of course) he has listed his celebrity crushes as: his *Summerland* co-star Lori Loughlin; Leslie Mann, with whom he acted in *17 Again*; singer and X-factor star Paula Abdul, who gave him the star necklace that he often wears (it says 'Reach for the Stars' on it); and Hollywood actress Penélope Cruz, whom he said was the sexiest woman he saw at the Oscars this year – apparently 'even her cardboard cut-out in rehearsals looked hot!' He also says that he's totally star struck by Angelina Jolie, and that he 'turns into a fifth grader' every time he talks to her! We can safely assume that Zac is not alone in having this problem.

# D is for...

## Dancing

It's a surprise to anyone who has seen Zac in *High School Musical* or *Hairspray* that he doesn't find dancing easy at all. He looks like a complete natural on the dance floor but it doesn't come easily to him at all. He explains, 'I grew up being into sports and I wasn't trained to move my body in the right way for dancing.' He found some of the choreography for the *High School Musical* films very challenging, and was a bit daunted by the more complex moves in the third film, but thanks to his determination to fulfil the role and the professionalism he's famous for, it's hard to tell when watching the finished product that he struggled at all. But Zac says that his co-stars always got the moves right before he did, and he self-effacingly revealed that 'in rehearsals it's always, "OK, one more take for Zac."'

ZAC DURING A LIVE PERFORMANCE OF *HAIRSPRAY*.

But it seems that some of his co-stars are more impressed with Zac's dance skills than he's letting on. Claire Danes, who appeared with him in period drama *Me and Orson Welles*, says Zac can move very well and that he's a really co-ordinated guy. She says that taking dance lessons with Zac was 'very humbling' because he was such a quick learner.

# Dating

Zac says that he has always been shy around girls. Staff at his school say that he was never one for the ladies, and that he was rarely seen hanging around with girls. And Zac has said that at school there were three girls who were 'too tall and too pretty and kind of ruled the high school,' but he 'probably didn't say two words to them the whole time I attended the school.' He says that if he likes a girl, he'll blush and tell stupid jokes, and that this is how she can tell he's interested.

And does he have a type? 'I don't know the exact measurements but I like curvy girls – girls with hips,' he says. 'I'm also huge on legs. I love girls with nice, long, sexy legs.' But looks aren't everything. 'It's not all about what you look like, it's so much more. I

VANESSA AND ZAC ARE
REPORTED TO HAVE
BEEN DATING SINCE THE
FIRST *HIGH SCHOOL
MUSICAL* FILM.

know it sounds really cheesy but it's more about what's on the inside when you're dating a girl.'

And what sort of boyfriend is he? Well, he and Vanessa keep their relationship pretty private, but it does sound as though Zac tries to be gentlemanly – letting the girl choose the movie at the cinema and bringing her flowers on Valentine's Day.

# The Derby Stallion

*The Derby Stallion* (2007) was Zac's first feature film. It wasn't a huge commercial or critical success, but for an actor, the first starring role in a film is always a formative experience and this was no exception.

The film centres on Zac's character, Patrick McCardle, a small town kid who doesn't get on with his dad, and who finds it hard to make friends. The 'Derby Stallion' of the title is an injured racehorse, and Patrick is determined to rehabilitate him and return him to his former glory and, in the process, win the State Cup Steeplechase.

Although Zac was delighted to be offered the role, he did worry that he'd bitten off more than he could chew, because he lacked experience in one crucial area. 'I've never done any horseback riding,' he confessed to *Life Story* magazine. Zac thought the riding would be done by stuntmen, but no. He was told that he'd have three lessons and then he would be jumping. 'I guess that turned on my adrenaline,' he said. Never one to shirk a challenge, Zac threw himself into his role. 'I started focusing on horseback riding. Previously, horses were never something I thought I'd be interested in. The first time I got on the horse, I realised I was completely wrong. It's so thrilling and amazing to be on top of a horse.' The perseverance paid off – in the film, Zac looks like someone who has been riding his whole life rather than someone who has just had three lessons – even if it did come at the cost of some bumps and bruises!

# Dylan Efron

Zac has a very close relationship with his brother Dylan, who is four-and-a-half years younger than he is. When they were younger they used to fight all the time (often over who got to sit in the front seat of the car), but they get on very well now, and enjoy playing tricks on each other.

A few years ago he told a story about how his brother 'made me reach into a dark, scary hole to look for a golf ball he accidentally threw in. When I put my hand down there, he screamed "SNAAAAAAKE!" at the top of his lungs. I almost passed out in fear.' Apparently, Dylan thought this was hilarious. Zac has often said that he easily gets on the same wavelength as his kid brother — and that when they were children his parents preferred to describe this as Zac 'acting down' to Dylan's level.

Since Zac has been busy with his acting career and left the family home, he doesn't spend as much time with Dylan as he'd like to, and he says, 'Now I don't see him very often, I cherish the time I have with him.' But as Dylan gets older, the two brothers are seen out and about together from time to time, and Zac is clearly quite protective of Dylan when he feels that he needs to be. He told one interviewer, 'There have been a couple of times where I've been out with my younger brother and someone said a couple of words to him that were not nice, and I've had words back.'

# E is for...

## Education

Some of Zac's teachers have said that he was the class clown when he was at school, but Zac was also a good student and he certainly worked very hard at school. He modestly says that he wasn't particularly academically gifted, but he was certainly determined. He said that he would 'flip out' if he got Bs instead of As in his schoolwork, and sure enough, his determination paid off and he left school with a grade point average of 4.3 – all A

Zac answers questions during a film première.

grades, no less. His favourite subject at school was English, and he still enjoys reading and does some writing in his spare time.

It's a bit of a surprise to learn that, unlike Troy Bolton, his character in *High School Musical*, Zac wasn't the coolest guy in his high school. 'I was just average. I worked hard in school, got good grades,' he says. The secretary at his high school agrees with Zac's assessment. 'I don't remember Zac being popular,' recalls Joyce Hartwig. 'He wasn't exactly the school heart-throb, you never saw him with girls.' She says she thinks that the time Zac spent away from school at the theatre, and the individual tutoring he needed to take so that he could catch up, meant that he had fewer opportunities to mingle with his peers.

A former classmate adds to this picture: 'He was a very sensible kid, a bit nerdy. He didn't hang out with the cool crowd. He always studied hard but wasn't around that much.' He went on to say that Zac got a bit of a hard time over his acting. 'Zac never knew how to handle the kids who teased him. He wasn't bullied constantly, but for him it made going to class very difficult.' Zac doesn't dwell on the difficulties that came from mixing high school with his acting career. 'I wasn't bullied that bad or anything like that, but I just wasn't like the "it" guy at school,' he says.

But did he ever get in trouble? It certainly sounds like it! 'Yeah, I looked at a couple of papers, taking tests, stuff like that, it was small things,' he confesses. He also told an interviewer about his most embarrassing moment at school, which occurred in Spanish class. 'I was going to write up a sentence on the board and my pants fell down in front of the class. Everyone was laughing, it wasn't a big deal, but the teacher got really flustered and upset and sent me home. It was a "wardrobe malfunction", for sure!'

# Entourage

*Entourage* is a comedy-drama TV series that has appeared on the HBO channel since 2004. It's about a young film star from New York and his adventures (and misadventures) as he gets used to the unfamiliar surroundings of Hollywood. One of the co-producers is Mark Wahlberg and the plot is loosely based on his experiences of moving from New Kids On The Block fame to working as a serious actor. Because of the Hollywood setting, one of the quirks of the show is that there are lots of celebrity cameos and guest appearances – at least one star joins in the

*ENTOURAGE* STAR MARK WAHLBERG.

fun per episode. The list of celebrities who have been invited to appear on the show reads like a *Who's Who* of Hollywood. And in the Season Six episode 'Security Briefs', which aired in September 2009, Zac made an appearance as himself. He is the unwitting cause of tension when one of the characters steals him as a client – from someone who isn't at all happy about it! Zac's section of the show was filmed in the Nike shop in Beverly Hills and a member of staff said that he was 'really nice'.

# ER

One of Zac's 'big break' appearances on TV was in the hit show *ER*. He landed a small guest-starring role in the show in 2003, playing Bobby Neville. Bobby is a teenage boy who comes into the ER with gunshot injuries, and despite the doctors' best efforts (including cracking open his chest) he sadly dies. Despite this being a small role for Zac, it was clearly one of the roles that brought him to the attention of casting directors.

Fortunately, Zac's real-life trip to the ER had a much happier outcome. In January 2008, he was rushed to the Cedars-Sinai Medical Centre in Los Angeles, suffering from acute appendicitis. While he was shooting *17 Again*, he began to suffer from excruciating stomach pains, but kept on working for the whole day anyway. 'I was sitting in-between takes, just off set, debating whether or not an alien was going to pop out of my stomach,' said Zac afterwards. Fortunately, he was taken to hospital in time. He had to have an emergency operation to remove his appendix, and happily it all went smoothly and Zac quickly made a full recovery. He got back to work as soon as he could – 'I was one organ lighter, but I had to get back' – because he didn't want to risk the film finishing late. What a star!

## Fame

Zac often talks about how much he loves being an actor, how much he enjoys the constant challenges, the new skills he learns, and the relationships he builds with co-stars and directors. He's also very proud of the films he has made, but there are times when he does find some of the pressures of being famous difficult to deal with. 'I wouldn't change anything for the world,' he says, 'although the fame part of this industry is tough to handle at times. I can

71

tell you that fame is probably the most un-adorable thing about acting. *High School Musical* is what got me here today and I'm very grateful – but the fame part isn't so fun.' He has no regrets though, and he is prepared to take the rough with the smooth – 'it's unnerving at times and it's a little bit scary at moments, and it can start to feel invasive, but I just remember every day that this is a small price to pay,' says Zac, with his usual lack of ego.

Zac thinks that the fact that he lives a relatively normal life, and has close relationships with friends and family, is what helps him cope with the continual pressures of this 'un-adorable' side of the business. He's aware that many stars jeopardise their careers and their relationships, whether it's through drink, drugs, fighting with photographers, partying too hard or developing an attitude, you name it, and he's determined not to go down that road.

But despite Zac feeling that his life is as normal as he can make it, it's clear that the day-to-day issues he faces are not things that we can easily imagine. He was once asked in an interview by *Time* magazine what he'd do if, for one day, he wasn't famous. And what he chose was something that most people have the opportunity to do quite often. 'I'd like to not have anything planned out – see where the day takes me,' he said. 'Perhaps start driving and end up someplace completely different. That would be cool.' Not being able to do something that most of us take for granted is a price to pay for fame and fortune, which goes to show that life in Hollywood isn't always as perfect as we might imagine it to be.

Zac also knows that keeping out of the showbiz traps that catch so many unwary actors helps him cope with the constant pressures of the paparazzi. 'I think if I had more to hide, it would be more bothersome. At this point, I don't do too many things that I need ultra privacy for,' he says. He is totally upfront about the fact that he doesn't want to be chased about by photographers, and that he is becoming savvier about avoiding paparazzi. 'I'm definitely making leaps and strides in figuring out how to keep my head down, and that's completely liberating,' says Zac. 'You know, it's legal to take pictures, but it's also legal to hide.'

He also makes sure that he keeps his feet on the ground about being photographed all the time. 'Photos are just a frame of your life; they don't represent what kind of a person you are,' he says, wisely. Added to that, he's not especially sympathetic to other actors who court the press on the one hand and then complain about being snapped by the paparazzi on the other.

HOLLYWOOD ACTOR MATTHEW McCONAUGHEY.

'Matthew McConaughey has single-handedly funded the tabloid magazines for the past two years now. If he would put on a shirt and just get away from the beach, maybe there would be a few less paparazzi around,' said Zac, showing uncharacteristic impatience in one interview.

And is Zac ever tempted to read his own press, or look himself up on Google? Not really. He says that sometimes it can be a bit difficult to keep up with what people are saying in the gossip magazines, and most of the time there's so much nonsense published online that he doesn't even try to keep track. 'There can be a hundred tabloid articles written about me and I would never hear about them. I don't want to hear them. Nobody comes and tells me.' But there are some exceptions, like celebrity blogger Perez Hilton, who causes a bit of a nuisance for Zac! 'If Perez Hilton puts up one post, there is just a flood of incoming phone calls from friends and family to see if it's true and to see what the deal is.'

But surely there must be *some* advantages to being famous? Zac must be able to get privileged access to special places, or the best tables in restaurants, right? You would think so, but no, apparently not! Zac says that every time he even hints at special treatment, it backfires on him somehow: 'I was pulling into a parking garage to do press for a *High School Musical* movie. I didn't have any cash on me whatsoever. It was…three dollars to park. I told the parking guy: "Can I come in? I'm Zac. I'm a part of this movie. I'm in the film, I promise. I'm not lying." He was like: "Absolutely not. No. I've already heard that too much today." So [I say]: "People are saying they are me? I literally have a picture of me in the film right here." He was like: "Yeah, I'm not buying it." I had to go to a cash point machine!' So much for film stars getting everything for free and not having to carry cash!

# Fan mail

If you want to write a letter to Zac, you can send it to the address below:

Zac Efron
P.O. Box 960
Avila Beach, CA 93424
USA

He doesn't promise to reply to every letter (as you can imagine, there are rather a lot of them to keep up with!) but he does reply when he can. So, you never know, you may be one of the lucky ones who get a personal reply from Zac!

# Fans

Zac is always very appreciative of his fans, and this is demonstrated not only by the things he says in interviews, but in the way he has taken the time to respond to so many fan letters personally. He told the *Metro* newspaper that his fans were fun, and 'very energetic and supportive. There are none better.' In the early days, he had to change his phone number because the success of *High School Musical* took him a bit by surprise. He thinks it started because some younger kids at his school got hold of his mobile number and passed it around!

He is getting used to a change in his fan base – when he started out, they were mainly school children, but as he branches out into a wider range of films, he's dealing with a widening of his fan base too – he says that he is flattered by the way some older girls want to throw themselves at him, and now it's sometimes the mums that are the fans! Zac says that

ZAC HAS A FANTASTIC RELATIONSHIP WITH HIS FANS.

encounters with his older fans can be very interesting. 'They tend to get over-excited, even more so than the kids,' he reveals. 'Sometimes the kids won't even know who I am, and the parents want them to care! And the kids are not remotely interested in any way and the mums will start crying. And the kids really don't care.' He has said that in many ways he finds the young kids easier to deal with

– the older ladies can, it seems, come on a bit strong and Zac finds them a little bit intimidating!

When Zac visited the UK in 2008, there were reports all over the internet about an encounter with a scary fan who tried to attack him and shouted at him. But Zac was pretty calm about it and said at the time that it was all blown out of proportion – apparently he was totally unaware of the whole thing, until all his relatives started calling to find out what had happened.

With all the moving around he does, Zac notices differences in the way his fans behave in different countries. He says that in the UK, he has started to recognise a lot of the same girls who come to all the premières and events. He has talked about the almost scary premières in Latin America, and when he was in Sydney, he told a newspaper: 'I'd say Australia's probably a higher decibel level than, for instance, Japan. You know, Japan's a very quiet scream. It's a very polite, bowing scream... it's very excited but hush hush.'

But wherever he goes, Zac does appreciate his fans. He said, 'I'm very blessed – I have a very cool fan base. I don't know how I got so lucky. I'm still a bit amazed by all the attention.' Zac says that the effort that many of his fans put into supporting him is amazing: 'The banners! All jewelled and sparkly ones, I saw a woven one! And I thought: that must have taken weeks!' And what's the weirdest thing he has seen written on a banner? Well, apparently the oddest banner Zac has seen was held up by a man who was slightly older than the average fan, and it said, simply: 'WHERE'S VANESSA?' OK, then…

# Fears

There have been rumours circulating for a while that Zac is afraid of heights, but this certainly isn't the case. He happily went bungee jumping – and, we're told, added a little acrobatic manoeuvre for good measure – while on location in Canada for *Charlie St. Cloud* and he has long held an ambition to go skydiving. When he was in Hawaii for the Maui Film Festival, Zac and his brother Dylan jumped off a 30 foot cliff into a pool of cold water. Brrr! These don't sound like the actions of someone who is afraid of heights! But even though heights aren't a problem, this doesn't mean that Zac is totally without fears. He's not only confessed to being a bit scared of sharks, especially since he's been doing more surfing, but also zombies and the girl from *The Ring*. Perhaps it's time to lay off the horror movies for a little while then, Zac?

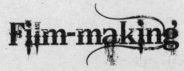

# Film-making

Zac is clearly enjoying being an actor at the moment, but he has long been interested in the wider art of film-making and the range of skills involved in making a movie. Before his acting career took off, he had been offered a place to study Film at the University of Southern California. He's rumoured to be taking a producer's credit in an upcoming project, and has said that he wants to try directing at some point. 'I want to be behind the camera,' he said early on in his career, but with typical modesty and lack of ego, he added: 'I'd like to make my mark in front of the camera before I endeavour to get behind it.' *Variety* magazine reported in February 2010 that Zac had signed a producer's deal with Warner Bros., so perhaps a behind-the-camera role isn't that far away?

Zac loves everything about being part of a film – not just the acting, although he says that's great fun, but everything that comes from being on the set. 'It's

ZAC ENJOYS EVERY PART
OF THE FILM-MAKING
PROCESS, FROM THE
ACTING TO JUST BEING ON
SET AND SEEING THE
WHOLE PROJECT COME
TOGETHER.

such a creative environment, all these people, all working in different ways, but all towards a common goal.' He knows that there are lots of factors that go into a successful movie, and that if one person slacks off or has an off day, this means that there's more work for everyone else to pick up. 'Making a movie is like trying to put together an amazingly intricate puzzle,' he says. But he loves the feeling of unity that comes from being on set, and it's clear that he has got his eyes and ears open and he's learning all he can about how movies are put together, and this can only stand him in good stead in the future.

# Firefly

Zac made his TV debut in 2002, in *Firefly*, a cult TV series created by Joss Whedon, the director behind *Buffy The Vampire Slayer* and *Angel*. The series starred Canadian actor Nathan Fillion as spaceship captain Mal Reynolds in a futuristic drama about how the human race survives after it is forced to abandon Earth. Zac appeared for just a few minutes in a flashback, playing the teenage version of one of the major characters, Simon Tam. His appearance in the

*FIREFLY* CREATOR JOSS WHEDON.

show may have been fleeting, but he clearly did enough to impress casting directors, as more TV roles followed before long.

# Food

Although he has acquired a reputation as a bit of a health freak, Zac is clearly a man who likes his food, and although he does try to eat healthily, he doesn't keep exclusively to health food. He happily admits to being willing to eat anything – he says he'll even blend steak and apples and drink the resulting goo for a dare – and lots of papers reported gleefully that he once ate some treats that Vanessa had bought for her dogs and left out on her kitchen counter. Zac was completely unfazed by the mistake, saying that the canine treats were 'good, if a little bland'!

But generally, his tastes in food are a little more conventional. He likes exotic food like sushi, but only when he's eating out, as he admits that he isn't much of a cook. Left to himself, he says that he keeps it simple, with macaroni cheese. He does like his treats, too. He has said that his favourite fast food is a sandwich of honey mustard chicken and bacon – and that his idea of heaven is being first in line when the samples of Krispy Kreme doughnuts are being handed out – so all in all, it's probably just as well that he likes to work out!

# Footloose

Zac had originally landed the starring role in a remake of the musical film *Footloose*, and was quoted as saying that he would like to add his 'own little bit of flair' to the role that had been made famous by Kevin Bacon in the 1984 original. But in March 2009 it was announced that Zac had dropped out of the film so that he could appear in the period drama *Me and Orson Welles* instead. When asked about his decision to leave *Footloose*, he explained that he was worried about becoming typecast. He felt that doing another musical straight after the *High School Musical* films and *Hairspray* wasn't going to be enough of a challenge, and he wanted to keep things fresh. 'It was a fantastic idea, but this is a big moment for me and I'd like to use it to try new things. I have that opportunity, and who knows – I don't want that to disappear,' he said.

OPPOSITE: ZAC WAS MOOTED TO PLAY REN MCCORMACK IN THE REMAKE OF *FOOTLOOSE*, PLAYED BY KEVIN BACON IN THE 1984 ORIGINAL.

# G is for...

## Gadgets

Zac's love of video games is well known, with rumours circulating that Vanessa is threatening to make him get rid of his games consoles because she barely sees him. He also is a heavy user of his mobile phone, sending and receiving thousands of text messages every month. He is a big fan of Apple products – he was one of the first to get an iPhone and he makes sure that he gets the updated versions. But like a lot of guys, he likes to keep up with the latest gadgets and his current favourite is the Apple iPad, which he says he can't leave alone. 'I'm all about the iPad. There's something about the multi-touch interface. It's less cumbersome than a laptop and I think it has cool games and apps. I am totally geeking out about it.' Yes, it certainly sounds like it!

# Good causes

Zac is ready to get involved with a good cause – as are many stars. But the list of good causes that Zac has supported in the last few years is pretty impressive by any standards. He does regular work for Habitat for Humanity, a charity which is involved with disaster relief and also combating homelessness in the United States. He is also involved with the Make-A-Wish Foundation, who aim to grant the wishes of children who have life-threatening medical conditions, 'to enrich the human experience with hope, strength, and joy.' Anna Ruter was diagnosed with a rare metabolic condition when she was eight days old, and she met Zac through the foundation a couple of years ago, when she was 10. 'I was shaking inside when I saw him near the table,' Anna said. 'He has blue eyes, he has freckles and he is funny.' The third charity that Zac regularly supports is Music for Relief, which responds to natural disasters as they occur to help victims recover and rebuild, with an emphasis on housing, education programs and resources, and also campaigns on climate change.

As well as these regular commitments, Zac will also pitch in to help for one-off fundraisers. In January 2010, in the aftermath of the Haiti earthquake, he and Vanessa joined George Clooney's Hope for Haiti Now telethon to raise funds by being part of the celebrity phone-bank which took pledges from callers. They were joined in the phone bank by dozens of stars, including *High School Musical* co-star Ashley Tisdale, veteran actors Jack Nicholson and Robert De Niro… and Zac's crush, Penélope Cruz. The event raised $58 million for disaster relief.

Career Gear, a charity that helps men from disadvantaged backgrounds find a job and stay in employment, held a fundraiser in May 2010, for which Zac donated a tie – although his self-confessed fondness for accessories might have made it hard to part with one!

In December 2008, our favourite actor played Santa Claus and took toys to a LA children's hospital, spending two hours giving out the presents, signing

ZAC AND SURFER TOM WHITAKER CHAT ON BONDI BEACH.

autographs and posing for pictures. One of the children's parents said at the time, 'The kids were smitten and beaming from ear to ear. Some of the kids couldn't even speak, but they had the widest grins and would sit as close to him as possible. Zac was super gracious and could not have been more kind and truly happy to be there.'

Zac also combined charity work with his love of surfing when he took part in a fundraising surf session on Australia's Bondi Beach in aid of The OneSight Foundation, which helps people in developing countries to have access to free eye care. It was, we're told, a very popular session – especially with young girls. Can't think why this would be…

And if there weren't enough good causes to be involved in at home, Zac also took the time to record a fundraising message for the UK's Children in Need appeal, telling viewers that 'even a few pennies can make a difference.'

# H is for...

## Hair

For a long time, Zac's trademark hairstyle was a bit long with a fringe that flopped over his eyes – the style that became familiar from his character in *High School Musical*. But the time came when he had to make a break and move on to a new hairstyle – and that time came with *Hairspray*. Zac had modelled the character of Link Larkin on a young Elvis – so obviously a fairly radical change of hairstyle was called for. Zac had his hair cut short and slicked

ZAC'S LONG HAIR
BECAME A SIGNATURE
OF TROY BOLTON IN
*HIGH SCHOOL
MUSICAL*, BUT HE HAS
SINCE CUT IT FOR A
NEATER LOOK.

back, and found it quite an odd experience. 'It was the first time I felt clippers on my head since I was in seventh grade. I was like, "Omigod. I can feel my scalp." And I had ears. I was like, "Damn, they got big."' But despite the shock of suddenly having short hair (and ears), Zac did enjoy changing his look for a film role.

Since then, Zac has definitely chosen to go the low-maintenance route, saying that he spends 30 seconds on his hair in the morning. 'If I've got an event, a lady will put cream in it but other than that it just lays there,' he says. He also revealed the secret of his perfectly mussed-up hairstyle in an interview with *Time* magazine: 'Shower before you go to bed, and then sleep on your wet hair. Towel-dry it. In the morning, it's all messed up naturally.'

# Hairspray

Zac was cast in a starring role in the 2007 remake of John Waters's popular 1988 movie, *Hairspray*, the film that had first brought chat show host Ricki Lake to the big screen. The original had been a cult classic, but the new version was to reach a much wider audience,

NIKKI BLONSKY AND JOHN TRAVOLTA, ZAC'S CO-STARS OF THE HIT
MUSICAL *HAIRSPRAY*.

becoming the fourth highest grossing musical film in American cinema history.

The story is a musical set in 1962. Tracy Turnblad (Nikki Blonsky) is a cheerful, plump high school student who loves to dance and dreams of appearing on *The Corny Collins Show*, a dance extravaganza shown by the local TV station. Against the odds, she becomes one of the dancers, and despite not being one of the 'cool kids', wins the heart of Link Larkin, played by Zac. It isn't just a light and frothy dance flick, though – the film also addresses the serious topics of racial segregation and civil rights that formed some of the defining features of the 1960s. John Travolta and Michelle Pfeiffer also starred in the film – John Travolta taking a departure from his usual form and appearing as Tracy's mother!

At first, director Adam Shankman didn't think Zac was right for the part of Link, thinking that his Disney background gave him an image that was too clean-cut for the actor who was to play the slightly 'rough diamond' love interest. But Zac was determined to prove that he could bring what he called 'a little bit more edge' to the role, and after a series of auditions, he finally landed the part.

Despite having to cut and dye the hairstyle that had become his trademark, and put on around a stone in weight for the part, Zac loved being part of *Hairspray*, telling journalists, 'I love the musical trend right now. It's a dream project. I feel like it's a whole different skill set you get to prepare for a film.' He also enjoyed playing Link, because, 'you're allowed to be kooky. You're allowed to be weird, and allowed to be fun.' He found Link an interesting character because he's not a typical hero. 'He's a little bit shallow, a little bit self-absorbed. But ultimately pretty funny and cool, so I dig it.' One of Zac's favourite things about the 1960s is that it was the decade which saw the real emergence of rock and roll. To Zac, Elvis Presley defined 1960's rock and roll so he decided that he should base Link Larkin on Elvis. Because of this, he practiced thrusting his hips Elvis-style at home in front of his mirror!

# Heroes

In 2009, Zac came second in a poll to find out whom British youngsters thought of as their heroes. Only *Harry Potter* author J.K. Rowling got more votes than Zac did! But who does Zac consider to be his heroes? Well, he's admired Leonardo DiCaprio for a long time

*WOLVERINE* STAR HUGH JACKMAN.

and was glad when they got to meet and Zac was able to ask the older star for some advice. He also thinks that Jack Nicholson would be a great person to act alongside, and counts Christian Bale and Johnny Depp among his acting heroes. He'd like to work with director Zack Snyder, too, some day. But he says the person he would most like to speak to is veteran British actor Sir Ian McKellen – he even has Sir Ian's number in his phone!

As far as role models go, as well as Leo DiCaprio, Zac has expressed admiration for Australian actor Hugh Jackman, who is famous for starring in *Wolverine*. He admires Hugh's versatility and his ability to make different styles of films without being typecast into certain roles. 'He has this whole thing figured out,' Zac said in an interview with Australian media. 'What I enjoy about Hugh's career is that he is regarded as a mainstream, talented film actor and he's in action franchises... he's a stud. But then also, on the side, he's a fantastic song-and-dance man. You can tell he's put work into it. How he can maintain both and not be stereotyped as one or the other is hard work and I admire him for that.'

# High School Musical

Of course, as we all know, it was *High School Musical* which brought our favourite actor to the wider attention he deserved. Released on 20 January 2006, it quickly became the most successful movie that the Disney Channel has ever produced, with nearly 8 million viewers watching the US première and a huge craze for everything *High School Musical*, and everything Zac, following hard on its heels.

It seems incredible now that we know the film as a worldwide sensation, but 'High School Musical' was just the working title for the film. The producers hoped to come up with a better name for the project, but despite all their efforts, nobody could think of one, so the producers had to go for *High School Musical* – and nobody ever looked back!

*High School Musical* is set at East High School, and is a story about two high school juniors from rival cliques. Zac, of course, plays Troy Bolton, the popular captain of the basketball team, and Vanessa Hudgens takes the role of Gabriella Montez, an attractive but shy student who joins the school, and who is a whizz at maths and science. They meet on holiday, part, and then are reunited when Gabriella joins Troy's school.

ASHLEY, ANTON, VANESSA AND ZAC AT THE PREMIÈRE OF THE FIRST
*HIGH SCHOOL MUSICAL* FILM IN 2005.

Together, they try out for the lead parts in their High school musical, and shock the rest of the school – who would think that a sporty boy and a shy, nerdy girl would want to take part in a musical, let alone be fantastic at it and bag the starring roles? Despite attempts by other students to ruin their chances – either because, like Sharpay Evans (Ashley Tisdale), they want the parts for themselves or because they don't want their friends to change – Troy and Gabriella resist all the peer pressure and, along the way, manage to inspire others in the school to nurture their talents and follow their dreams.

Since its first release, the film has gained tremendous popularity all over the world, and *High School Musical* has now been seen by over 225 million people and counting. As if this were not enough, the DVD of the film (released on 23 May 2006) created a sales record by selling 1.2 million copies in its first six days. It became the fastest-selling television movie of all time – it seems that there are a lot of people who can't get enough of Zac and co.!

One of the main attractions behind the whole *High School Musical* phenomenon was obviously the music, and the soundtrack was the best-selling album in the United States for 2006. The success of the music was immediate. Shortly after *High School Musical* first aired,

Zac was credited on two songs in the Billboard Hot 100 at the same time: 'Get'cha Head in the Game' and the duet with Vanessa, 'Breaking Free'. By the following week, they were joined in the chart by three more songs from the film, all of them featuring Zac: 'Start Of Something New', 'What I've Been Looking For' and 'We're All In This Together'.

There were some people who disputed Zac's singing ability – despite his long track record in stage musicals – when it emerged that Drew Seeley's voice was blended with his on the soundtrack of *High School Musical*. But Zac told *Rolling Stone* magazine that this wasn't because he couldn't sing – the songs had been written for a tenor before he was cast as Troy, and his baritone voice was too deep for the parts. He did all his own singing in later movies, when the songs could be written for him, which must have gone a considerable way to silencing his critics! Even so, Zac has repeatedly told interviewers that although he enjoys musicals, he wants to concentrate on dramatic acting, rather than roles that are based more on singing.

*High School Musical* wasn't just a runaway success with audiences, attracting millions of devoted fans; it also wowed the critics and bagged a clutch of awards. Along with the Billboard Music Award for Soundtrack Album of the Year, it also bagged two Emmys – one for Outstanding Children's Program and the other for director Kenny Ortega, for Outstanding Choreography. Zac landed the Teen Choice Award for TV Breakout Star, and he and Vanessa won another Teen Choice Award for Best Chemistry!

Not bad at all for a project that Zac had accepted with what he describes as 'low expectations'! He has no doubt that *High School Musical* was popular not because of hype or marketing, but because the audience related to it and genuinely loved it. 'It wasn't the hype that made the movie,' he told the *Toronto Star*, 'it was the fans who took control. That's what I love.' He also thinks the film has a valuable message to convey to its young audience as well as the more obvious fun and frivolity: 'What's really important in life is following your dreams and truly being yourself.'

Zac also enjoyed the process of making the *High School Musical* films, largely because he got on so well with the rest of the cast. 'I think all of us came together and when we clicked on set – that was when I started to realise that this thing could be big. We all got along so great, and we all came together. In that moment, before we started filming, our connection on set just really made the movie what it is,' he said.

# High School Musical 2

After the enormous success of the first *High School Musical* film, Disney wasted no time in producing a sequel. In the second instalment, Zac's character, Troy Bolton, faces the normal stresses of teenage life – getting a summer job, worrying about how he'll meet the cost of going to college and, of course, making sure that he and Gabriella (Vanessa Hudgens) are able to stay together all summer. And as if this isn't enough to keep him busy, he has to deal with the scheming of Sharpay Evans (Ashley Tisdale), who wants Troy for herself!

The world première for the film was held at Disneyland on 17 August 2007. Most of the stars, including Zac, attended. The film was shown on American and Canadian television on the same day. More than 18 million people watched the première in the United States alone – 10 million more than the first film – making it the most watched Disney Channel film ever made, the most-watched 'made for cable' film ever and, at the time, the most watched telecast ever – surpassing the record that had previously been held by a massive American football game!

A WAXWORK VERSION OF TROY BOLTON.

The film was generally well-received by the critics as well as the fans. *USA Today*'s Robert Bianco described *High School Musical 2* as 'sweet, smart, bursting with talent and energy, and awash in innocence.' *High School Musical 2* won the Teen Choice award for Best Movie and an ALMA award for its director, Kenny Ortega. It was also nominated for two Emmy awards, as well as a host of others.

Zac enjoyed making the second film as much as he had the first, saying that he found the subject matter easy to relate to. 'High school is such a defining point in your history,' he said. 'Everyone remembers high school. There is so much drama and so many funny stories and great things happen. It shapes who you are.'

# High School Musical 3: Senior Year

The runaway success of the first two *High School Musical* films, when they were shown on the Disney television channel meant that when the time came for a third instalment, Disney decided to up the stakes this time. They decided to make a big budget film to be released in cinemas, rather than another film made for television. Like the previous films, *High School Musical 3* was a runaway success, making $42 million in its first three days! This was a new record for the largest opening weekend for a musical film.

This third part of the story follows Troy and the rest of the East High gang as they face the prospect of going their separate ways after they graduate from high school and move on to college. Joined by the rest of their friends at the school, they decide to stage an elaborate spring musical which will reflect their experiences together at school, and share their hopes and dreams – as well as their fears – about the future. The film got some good reviews – the *Telegraph* reviewer was impressed with the improvements that came from the bigger budget of a cinema release, saying that it 'injected colour, scale and visual depth.' But most of all, the critics loved Zac. *Entertainment Weekly* positively gushed: 'The beauty of Efron's performance is that he's a vibrant athletic hoofer who leaps and clowns with the heart-throb vigour of a young Gene Kelly, yet he's also achingly sincere. His fast-break alertness makes him the most empathetic of teen idols; he's like a David Cassidy who knows how to act, and who can swoon without getting too moist about it.' Wow! Zac must have been pleased

HIGH SCHOOL MUSICAL 3 WAS RELEASED IN 2008, THREE YEARS AFTER THE ORIGINAL FILM FIRST APPEARED ON THE DISNEY CHANNEL

with that, given that Gene Kelly has been one of his idols for years.

Along with the good reviews came more awards. Zac was voted Best Male Performance at the 2009 MTV awards and Choice Actor: Music/Dance at the 2009 Teen Choice Awards for his role in the film.

Zac clearly enjoyed his time making *High School Musical 3*, and found that even on the third instalment, there were still challenges to be faced and things to learn. 'I learned loads! I couldn't believe how much they stepped up the choreography and the music and everything.' He said that the atmosphere was very special, probably because the cast all knew each other so well and had got used to working together over the course of making the three movies – and they knew that this would be the last time they would all be together, which made it rather bittersweet: 'I think we found the delicate balance between work and play on the set of *High School Musical 3*. We kept it interesting and had fun, but we also worked very hard and that's something that's very difficult to achieve. Usually, you either work too hard or have too much fun on a movie set – but we did both. I think we perfected that.'

The cast have all talked about the special bond they had formed, and many of them admitted to bursting into tears when filming ended.

# High School Musical: The Concert

After the runaway success of the first *High School Musical* film, came the live show. *High School Musical: The Concert* was a 40-city concert tour that ran through the US and Latin America in 2006 and 2007, featuring live performances of several of the hit songs from the first film. Corbin Bleu, Ashley Tisdale, Lucas Grabeel, Monique Coleman and Vanessa Hudgens all took part in the tour, but Zac wasn't able to, because he was busy filming *Hairspray* at the time.

Instead, Drew Seeley, who had provided the original vocals for Troy's character in the film, took the role of Troy for the tour. Although he was genuinely busy on another project, it does seem as though Zac was quite glad to have an excuse to miss the tour, saying in a moment of extreme honesty: 'If I had to hear the *High School Musical* songs any more, I would have jumped off something really tall.' Perhaps you really can have too much of a good thing...

# High School Musical on Stage!

In the wake of the *High School Musical* sensation, lots of students wanted to stage their own High School Musicals – and so *High School Musical on Stage* was born! A rock musical version of the movie was adapted for stage, and after a year-long US tour staged by Disney along with a host of regional premières, it became a very popular choice for high school theatre productions, especially as there were two versions to choose from: a full length production and a shorter, 70-minute version. Similar stage adaptations of *High School Musical 2* followed, and have also been popular.

Sometimes when Zac meets fans they tell him that they are appearing in their own *High School Musical* show – and he tells an amusing story about it: Once he asked a young fan who had told him that she was playing Gabriella if the boy playing Troy was a good-looking guy. 'It's a girl,' she replied. It seems it's not just mixed schools who want to get in on the act!

OPPOSITE: *HIGH SCHOOL MUSICAL* BEING PERFORMED ON STAGE IN LONDON.

# Horoscope

Zac was born on 18 October 1987 which means that his star sign is Libra, but he's on the cusp with Scorpio. According to astrologers, this means that he has a magnetic personal charm and will be excellent at manoeuvring situations to get what he wants from them. People with this star sign work hard in their careers and apply themselves wholeheartedly to the pursuit of their goals. They are also, apparently, skilful at dealing with people, but punctuality is not their strong point. Well, we don't know about punctuality, but the rest certainly sounds like the Zac we love.

# House

For as long as he could, Zac was based at his family home in Arroyo Grande, but eventually he needed to move to Los Angeles to keep up with his work, and so he bought himself a house. Zac says that he hasn't gone all out on a huge 'Hollywood star' type house, but went for something modest and unpretentious, and describes his house as 'very modern, very clean, very simple.'

Small or not, Zac clearly enjoyed settling in to his new pad, choosing furniture and making the place his own – he even used to get talking about furniture shops with photographers on photo shoots! He liked having the clean, uncluttered look – partly so he could skateboard inside the house! 'It's got concrete floors, so I can't screw it up,' he told *Interview* magazine.

# I is for...

## Internet

Zac finds a lot of the online fandom surrounding him very odd and difficult to get used to. He has said that he keeps away from the film website IMDB.com because he finds so much of the commentary on the boards to be needlessly negative. He does find the enormous amount of online attention hard to get used to, because he thinks of himself as just a normal guy. 'People go online to look at my pictures. And people sign on to have chats about me!' he said, clearly

finding the idea that people are interested in him hard to take in. 'It's so alien. It's really weird. It all gets a little blown out of proportion. Not that I don't enjoy it, but it's a weird feeling and kind of hard to describe.'

Zac takes his privacy incredibly seriously, and tries to keep details about his personal life off the internet as much as possible. There have been lots of Twitter feeds that claim to be Zac's, but he wants us all to know that every single one of them is a fake. Zac has decided to let the social networking aspect of the communication revolution pass him by, and has opted out of Twitter, Facebook, MySpace – the lot. He told fans: 'I kind of value people not knowing where I am or what I'm doing.' He added, 'So if you [find] me, it's a poseur, don't talk to him. And Vanessa doesn't have any of them, either. None.' So, now you know – without that Twitter feed, you'll have to find other ways to keep up with our favourite star.

# Interview Magazine

Zac is used to the camera, and quite accustomed to having his photograph taken. But when he agreed to a shoot for *Interview* magazine in 2009, it turned out to be a bit of a different experience. This photo shoot was a far cry from the squeaky-clean promotional photos of Zac's recent past: these arty black-and-white shots were definitely a more 'grown up' style of picture.

Zac enjoyed the experience, saying that the photographer was 'very cool and I saw what he wanted to do.' And what he had to do was roll around in a load of wet sand. 'There was, like, a giant sandbox in the middle of a studio, and then I just got to roll around in the dirt for a couple of hours. I got pretty dirty by the end of it, so that was fun.' But there wasn't just sand in the sandbox. There was also a beautiful model called Edita Vilkeviciute, and she wasn't wearing any clothes. So, how did that go? 'It just kind of happened,' said Zac. He said that working with Edita wasn't awkward. 'She was so professional. It wasn't really up to me so I just kind of rolled with it', which perhaps wasn't the best choice of words given the resulting pictures…

The pictures were a huge departure from Zac's previous image, and they caused a media firestorm, with some critics saying that they were inappropriate and 'too sexy' for someone like Zac who had young fans. But Zac was completely unapologetic about the photo shoot and rejected the idea that there was anything wrong with the shots, saying that they were artistic pictures taken by a photographer he respected. 'You're never going to please everybody,' Zac said. 'I'm growing up. That's the way it is.'

And what was Zac's girlfriend's reaction when she saw these photos of her bloke rolling around with another girl? 'Damn,' Vanessa told *Access Hollywood* when she saw the pictures. 'They're sexy.' Vanessa has said before that she thinks it's important not to be a jealous girlfriend – and from this, it looks as though she practises what she preaches.

# Isle of Man

When Zac went to film *Me and Orson Welles* on the Isle of Man, he was really looking forward to the idea of peace and quiet. 'I was looking forward to that seclusion. From what I'd heard it was a pretty quiet place and there weren't a lot of people there. I can't tell you how appealing that sounded,' he said. He was hoping that filming the movie somewhere relatively isolated would provide a bit of a contrast from the high pressured atmosphere of Los Angeles – somewhere where he could kick back a bit and not

ZAC IS MOBBED BY FANS AT THE PREMIÈRE OF *ME AND ORSON WELLES*.

have to worry about the constant scrutiny he has to deal with at home.

But sadly, it was not to be. News of Zac's arrival soon got out, and almost immediately the quiet, sleepy Isle of Man was besieged by fans and turned into what Zac's co-star Claire Danes called 'the Isle of Teenage Girls', so his dream of seclusion was shattered. Every move he made was followed by hordes of fans, and after filming he had to be taken back to his hotel in a police car! The hotel was surrounded with fans chanting, 'We want Zac' day and night, so they ended up not being able to go out much after all. Claire said she'd never seen anything like it. 'I'd never worked with anyone so famous,' she wrote in *Time* magazine.

# J is for...

## John Travolta

Zac appeared with John Travolta in *Hairspray*, and found the experience of working with another actor who'd made his name in musicals – including *Grease*, one of Zac's favourites – very exciting. But John had moved away from his usual style for this movie – appearing in *Hairspray* as a larger than life... *lady*. Nobody was absolutely sure how this was going to work, but Zac says that John got into the role of Tracy's mother Edna immediately, and that everyone

was really impressed with how convincing he was, and that he galvanised everyone into action. 'John came into the room and everyone was there – the whole cast, the producers – in his costume and make up,' said Zac. 'On every person's face – it was just knowing that we could really pull it off. We just turned around and started going for this film.' John Travolta may have made his name in musical films, but he has gone on to make a huge range of other films, from comedy to action movies, and Zac said that he would love to follow a similar path. 'I could only dream. I would hope so. That would be very cool,' he said, adding, 'I need to find a white three-piece suit!'

Zac says that he really admires Travolta's attitude to the parts he plays, the way he just gives a part everything he's got. 'The others are as cool as John, but it's the confidence with which he approaches everything – he just knows that he is cool,' said Zac. 'You even see a little bit of it in Edna. It's so iconic, and I'll always admire his courage, the way he always goes for it. It's marvellous.'

OPPOSITE: ZAC'S *HAIRSPRAY* CO-STAR, JOHN TRAVOLTA.

# Jonny Quest

One of the things that Zac's working on at the time of writing is a feature film called *Jonny Quest*. Warner Bros has confirmed that the film is in production and is expected to be released in 2012 – and that Zac has signed on to take the title role.

The film is to be based on a popular 1960s animated Hanna–Barbera TV series. The stories revolved around a young boy who travels the world with his scientist father, his adopted brother from India, Bandit the bulldog, and a government agent, called Bannon, who is assigned to protect them as they go on their adventures investigating scientific mysteries. In this new version, the timeline will have moved on from the original, and Jonny will be an adult rather than 11 years old.

Zac has been careful not to say too much about the film and says the project is in its early stages. 'It's a long, long process. It's so hard when people start leaking titbits. They're very, very early on [with it]. Not that it won't happen; it's just early,' he says.

Zac was a bit of a surprise choice for the role, and not everyone thinks that updating the timeline with an adult Jonny will work out – but there are some commentators who think that updating the series with an older Jonny will make the story more effective and believable, and that it could be a good choice of role for Zac, and take him one step further on from his *High School Musical* days.

# Judaism

Zac comes from a Jewish family – his surname is the Hebrew word for 'lark'. But although he is ethnically Jewish, he doesn't practise the Jewish religion. He describes himself as an agnostic – someone who is undecided about whether there is a God or not. He told *Rolling Stone* magazine in 2007 that his parents had chosen to raise him in an agnostic way – with a respect for religion and a strong personal code, but without practising any particular faith.

# K is for...

## Kenny Ortega

*High School Musical* director Kenny Ortega has been described by the cast as the 'cornerstone' of the films. He had previously choreographed the 1987 hit *Dirty Dancing*, and directed some episodes of *Gilmore Girls*, which had been a huge hit with a teenage audience. Ortega says that he knew from the beginning of the *High School Musical* project that Zac was special, and compares him to one of Zac's heroes, Leonardo DiCaprio. 'I met Leo at the beginning of his dramatic

*HIGH SCHOOL MUSICAL* DIRECTOR KENNY ORTEGA.

transition,' says Kenny. 'Everybody in town wanted him... It was very familiar, meeting with Zac. The well runs deep with him.'

Kenny thinks that Zac has a lot to offer, not just because of his talent but also because of his personality and his sense of fun. He said: 'From the moment that they walked in the door there was a real sort of life going on and an interesting individual, somebody who just didn't want to act but has a life and is going to be fun. Because he's colourful as an individual, he's going to have a lot to draw on.' Ortega also appreciates Zac's intelligence and thinks it's a real asset to him in his career. 'He's also one of the brightest actors I've ever had the chance to work with at 20 years old, and he keeps me on my toes. I think it's about that. It's about actors that bring something with them other than the craft,' he says.

# Kisses

Zac and Vanessa, understandably, both take pains to keep their personal life very much to themselves, so we don't know much about it. But Zac has to do a fair amount of kissing in the course of his acting career, and critics often pick up on the chemistry he manages to generate with his female co-stars. Of course, we know that the rapport between Troy and Gabriella in the *High School Musical* films was helped by Zac's off-screen relationship with Vanessa, but what of the other leading ladies?

It's well known that Ashley Tisdale found it very odd having to kiss someone she regarded as a close friend, and caused shock waves when she went on record as saying the kiss they shared when filming *Suite Life* was 'disgusting'. Taken aback by the furore that was kicked off by her comments, Ashley later explained her stance via Twitter. She admitted that 'maybe disgusting was the wrong word, but how would you feel kissing someone that's like your brother?' She then asked fans to suggest other adjectives she could use in future interviews – but she did set minds at rest by saying that despite the awkwardness, Zac was a good kisser!

During an interview for their film *Me and Orson Welles*, Claire Danes was asked what kissing Zac was like. 'Amazing,' she replied, adding that she also found it very easy to flirt with him. And Zac's *Summerland* co-star Kay Panabaker shared her very first kiss with Zac: 'Then I told him it was my first kiss ever,' said Kay. 'He said, "Really? I hope I didn't ruin it for you." And he didn't!' Awww.

ZAC HAS HAD PLENTY OF
ON-SCREEN KISSES WITH
OFF-SCREEN SWEETHEART
VANESSA HUDGENS.

# L is for...

## Leonardo DiCaprio

When Zac was a teenager, he didn't really like Leo DiCaprio all that much. His face was everywhere in the midst of *Titanic* fever, and Zac said that for a while he felt that he had been 'force-fed his image'. But as time went on, Zac became impressed by the way DiCaprio steadily changed the way he was perceived and ended up being cast in really meaty dramatic roles. 'But since then, through hard work and incredible performances and picking the right

LEONARDO DICAPRIO IS ONE OF ZAC'S BIGGEST INSPIRATIONS.

movies, he's completely "180'd" that and is one of my favourite actors,' Zac told *Time* magazine.

Perhaps Zac is aware that his squeaky-clean *High School Musical* image had been as pervasive as Leo's had been back in the days of *Titanic*. As Zac badly wants to make good choices so he can grow as an actor, it's natural that Leo is someone that he wanted to talk to, so he could pick his brains. He told *Entertainment Weekly* that he really wanted to be able to sit down with him, and with Johnny Depp, and ask their advice about his career. 'They do it because they love it, not because they enjoy being famous. You have to have good foresight and be really careful. If you don't adapt and learn at a very young age, you can really mess up,' Zac said of Johnny and Leo.

So, when he heard that the star of *The Aviator* and *Gangs of New York* was going to be appearing at the GQ Men of the Year event, he couldn't resist going along to the party just so he could see him. 'He was the only reason I went. I thought maybe I'd get to shake his hand,' explained Zac. Even stars get star struck, it seems! But for a while, it seemed as though Zac wasn't going to get to meet his idol. 'No one had seen Leo, and I was walking out and he walked right by. I was all, "Oh, hey!"' explained Zac. 'And he turned around and right there I had the 'in,' and I was like, "I just want to shake your hand, dude, I'm a big fan… I'd love to sit down and talk with you sometime." And he goes, "Right on.'"

That was a nice moment for Zac, and he was clearly thrilled to have met his idol. But things got even better when, shortly afterwards, they sat together at a LA Lakers basketball game and had a long talk. Zac found that Leo lived up to all his expectations, and gave him some sound advice. 'We talked the whole game, and he was just everything I thought he would be: smart, 'level headed', charming, hilarious. You know, the 'older-brother' vibe. That sounds so cheesy.' Cheesy or not, Zac clearly appreciated the opportunity for some guidance from an older star who had trodden the path that Zac is on – from teen idol to well-respected actor.

# Leslie Mann

Leslie was one of Zac's co-stars in *17 Again*. She played Scarlett, the wife of Zac's character Mike O'Donnell. The complication, of course, is that in the film, Leslie is married to the older version of Mike, played by Matthew Perry, and unbeknownst

ZAC'S *17 AGAIN* CO-STAR, LESLIE MANN.

to her, Mike has been returned to his 17-year-old self, played by Zac, and is going by the name of Mark. Confused?

So how did Zac deal with a role in which he had to be in love with a character so much older than he was? Well, at first, he was a bit worried about how he was going to make it look convincing, and found the idea of doing romantic scenes with his much older on-screen wife quite intimidating. 'I was wondering at the beginning— how is this gonna work?' he said in an interview with *Elle* magazine at the time. 'How am I gonna… you know…' Yes, Zac, we know! But when it came to it, it all worked out fine, because, 'by the end of the first rehearsal, I had such a big crush on Leslie, I didn't have to fake it.'

And how did the object of Zac's desire find working with him? Well, Leslie describes Zac as 'such a woman's fantasy'. Hmm. How about you tell us something we don't know, Leslie? She said that despite the 15-year age difference, 'It was hard not to be a lady cougar around him.' Rawwr! And Zac's love of a joke shows through in a story that Leslie tells about him. He had a bet with the director that he could get Leslie to give him her phone number, and got it by saying that he'd call her daughter on her birthday. Only once Leslie handed over her number was she let in on the joke: 'He turned to the director and said, "See, I told you I would get it."' Cheeky!

And could Zac imagine himself becoming romantically involved with an older woman, like his character in the movie did? Apparently so. 'I think, once you hit a certain age, age is irrelevant at some point,' he says.

# Los Angeles

Zac has bought what he describes as a 'modest' house in LA, and although he is fairly happy there, he has found that he has had to make a bit of an adjustment from the small beach town where he grew up. Most of his close friends still live there, so sometimes it has been a bit of a challenge to get used to the faster pace of life in Los Angeles. He said, 'LA is kind of a weird place for me because there are a lot of people. I have a lot to deal with.' In a town where stars are relentlessly pursued by hordes of paparazzi and everyone will flatter them to get what they want, it can be challenge for them to keep both feet on the ground.

ZAC IS GREETED BY FANS
AS HE ARRIVES HOME AT
LAX AIRPORT.

But Zac's confident that he can do it. 'I think I know what's real and what's not. I've been able to figure it out for myself and distinguish between the good and the bad that comes from living in Los Angeles,' he told interviewers at the Maui Film Festival. He's careful to try to make the most of the chances offered by living in Hollywood, without falling into the traps that so often catch younger actors. 'It's a tough balance. There's a lot of things you don't want to become involved with. But at the same time, opportunities abound.' He denies being squeaky clean – he's just sensible. 'I wasn't programmed by Disney,' he insists, in reference to his clean-cut background in his *High School Musical* days. 'It's common sense. If you're gonna be drunk with your friends, don't get wasted at the Chateau Marmont and hook up with some famous chick. It's not rocket science.' It does seem as though our favourite star knows how to stay grounded.

# Love

Zac has been with his long-term girlfriend Vanessa since they met during the filming of the first *High School Musical* film, and although he is famously cagey

Zac and Vanessa have been dating for nearly 5 years.

about discussing his relationship with her, he has talked quite a bit about the instant connection that they shared when they first met. So perhaps it was Vanessa he was thinking about when he said, 'I don't know if I believe in love at first sight, but of course I believe in two people having chemistry right away.'

Zac has been pretty clear in recent interviews that despite all the wedding and pregnancy rumours that seem to be constantly circulating on the internet, he's not looking to settle down and get into the marriage and babies scene just yet – and neither is Vanessa. After all, they're both still only in their early twenties. But Zac was asked about love and said, 'I don't know! I don't think you can describe the feeling. When you meet someone who makes you a better person and makes your life more fun…' So it does sound as though he and Vanessa have found something pretty special.

# Luck

Zac is well known for being down to earth and not at all hung up on the trappings of fame. Part of this seems to be because he truly believes that his success is largely down to luck. He's got plenty of talent, he's very good–

looking and he works incredibly hard – but, he says, the same could be said of lots of young actors who never make it. He describes actors like him as being 'a dime a dozen' and he firmly believes that once he starts thinking that he's special and that he can take success for granted, it'll all start to go wrong.

He says that this attitude largely comes from his upbringing – his parents made sure that he didn't get carried away by his acting work and that he kept up with his education. But even now he's hit the big time, he still isn't taking anything for granted – he still thinks that he's fortunate to have the opportunities, the fans, the wealth and the success that he's earned. Many of Zac's fans – and probably his directors and co-stars, too – might think that he's selling himself a bit short here, but there's no doubt that it's this down to earth attitude that makes so many people say that he's such a nice, normal person to work with.

# M is for...

## Marriage

Zac and Vanessa have been together for a few years now, so there are inevitable rumours about them. Nearly every week they are supposed to have split up, got together with other people, moved in together, be expecting a baby, or, of course, have got engaged or married. But Zac is very clear that he has no plans to settle down just yet. Marriage, in particular, will not feature on his to-do list for quite a while. He told GQ magazine in May 2009, 'I'm definitely not getting married. In this business, you're either getting married or they want you to be pregnant. I'm not getting married until I'm 40. If ever. The thought never crossed my mind...' Then he seemed to consider that he had a girlfriend who might get to read the interview, and amended his take on things slightly. 'Maybe not 40. Maybe not until I'm 30.'

And if marriage is off the cards, what about a family? 'Right now? No. Right now there's no more terrifying prospect than raising a family,' he says. 'I don't think I'm responsible enough, so I think that's years and years down the road.'

It sounds as though Vanessa isn't waiting around hoping for a Tiffany's box for a while, though. 'I think marriage and starting a family is great,' she says, 'but I'm so focused on my career right now that it doesn't really cross my mind.' Really, Vanessa? Not at all?

# Matthew Perry

Zac was excited to have the chance to work with Matthew Perry on *17 Again*, describing the *Friends* star as a 'comedic icon'. He said that part of the fun of the role was that he had to play the teenage version

MATTHEW PERRY IS SAID TO BE GOOD FRIENDS WITH ZAC.

of Matthew's character, and he found it really easy to imagine just what Matthew would have been like as a teenager! 'He was probably even more quick-witted and he probably had a really sharp tongue, and he was smart and sarcastic. Just younger!' said Zac. Was he tempted to just impersonate Chandler Bing from *Friends*? 'Sure, I could have done that all the time!' Zac says that Matthew has a very dry sense of humour and conveys this with a smirk rather than a wide smile, and he did his best to copy that expression for *17 Again*.

The pair had a really good relationship off screen, and they would discuss ideas in rehearsal. Zac says that Matthew helped him a lot as he developed his role, and he found himself calling him for advice a fair bit during filming. 'I would call and ask him what he thought and he would always come back with ideas, whether it was just a text or whatever – he would help out.' They didn't just talk about work, either – Zac admits that when they were talking about video games, Matthew recommended some new ones that Zac hadn't played – 'and I've got to be honest – he's actually better than me. I had all these questions for him, and the whole time he'd be "Dude, what video games are you playing?" And I thought, "This guy *is* 17 years old!"'

Matthew was asked in an interview if he'd like to go back to being 17 again, and he pointed at Zac and said, 'I'd love to be 17 again if I looked like this dude!' But Matthew did say that it wasn't just Zac's looks that made him right for the part – he also worked really hard. He's another of Zac's co-stars who respects his lack of ego and willingness to put the work in. 'He had no attitude – he was a good guy. He rolled up his sleeves and got to work,' said Matthew.

# Me and Orson Welles

In early 2008, Zac landed one of the lead roles in the film *Me and Orson Welles*, which was directed by Richard Linklater and based on a novel by Robert Kaplow. It was a bit of a departure from the style of movie that Zac had made previously, as it is set in the New York of the 1930s, and is based on the life of one of America's leading theatrical, film and literary figures of that period. This film, we discovered, was the new challenge that caused him to leave the cast of *Footloose*, and Zac described it as a 'completely different project than I've ever done before.' Zac wasn't especially relaxed about making such a different sort of film – one he describes as a 'coming of age story.' He was actually really nervous and says that he wondered if he'd bitten off more than he could chew. 'There wasn't a skill set I could fall back on,' he said. 'The other actors were incredibly accomplished. I was incredibly nervous. But usually it's a good sign if you're a bit scared at first.'

Zac has long admired the work of Orson Welles, ever since he was given the DVD of Welles's 1941 masterpiece *Citizen Kane* when he was 16. He said that before he made the film about Welles, he knew the classics – not just *Citizen Kane*, but *The Magnificent Ambersons* (1942) and the 1938 radio drama *War of the Worlds*. 'I thought I was well educated on this guy but I found out that I didn't know the first thing about him,' Zac admitted. He learned a lot while making the film, and has said that he hoped that the fact that he was taking part in the movie might encourage his younger fans to explore the work of the revered writer and filmmaker. 'I thought this was a good opportunity to reveal to them the genius that was Orson Welles,' he said. 'Perhaps the fans that don't know about Orson will have more of an opinion when they start to study him in school, a perspective and insight into the early life of this American icon.' In another interview he described Orson Welles as: 'A genius. A prodigy. An American icon. He owned virtually every medium, radio, theatre, film...'

In *Me and Orson Welles*, Zac plays the 'Me' of the title – a young man called Richard Samuels, who meets Orson Welles and is cast in his new production of Shakespeare's *Julius Caesar*. He meets, and eventually has an affair with, a gorgeous production assistant called Sonja, played by Claire Danes. Sonja is very ambitious and is more than happy to manipulate behind the scenes in order to succeed. Sonja and Richard spend the night together and Richard tells her that he loves her, but Sonja has her eye on her chance of a big break, and instead rejects Richard and sleeps with the director, Orson Welles. In the confrontation with Orson that follows, Richard is fired from the production. Orson eventually apologises and Richard comes back, only to be fired again after the first night. It turns out that Orson's apology was only to secure a successful first night performance – and that Sonja had been in on the deception all along. Hurt and betrayed, Richard gives up his hopes of acting and his love for Sonja, and returns to his family.

Zac told interviewers that when he took the role,

ZAC TAKES A BREAK FROM
FILMING *ME AND ORSON
WELLES* IN LONDON.

he was nervous about whether he could pull it off, and although he wanted a challenge and something that would 'shake things up' he did find the prospect a bit scary. But he needn't have worried – the film was very well received by the critics. Christian McKay's spot-on portrayal of Orson Welles got a lot of the attention, but Zac's performance was praised as well, with the *Telegraph* calling it 'very effective'. *Time Out* said that he played the role with 'an attractive, puckish energy,' and *Empire* clearly appreciated the undoubted chemistry between Zac and Claire Danes, describing Zac as 'striking sparks off leading ladies'. The change of direction seemed to pay off for Zac and hopefully will lead to some new challenges.

# Merchandise

When you add together *High School Musical* and Zac's personal following, there is an enormous range of merchandise available with his face on it, from notebooks and T-shirts to duvet covers and shoes.

Zac doesn't really understand a lot of the merchandising that goes on – he finds it all a bit baffling and doesn't really take it all in. He told *Nylon Guys* magazine, 'I try not to look at all of it. You can't enjoy or celebrate it; it's not a real thing,' which seems to be quite a wise viewpoint.

He says that the most bizarre item of merchandise he's seen was the *High School Musical* espresso cup. 'What kid is going to drink coffee out of a little *High School Musical* coffee cup?' he asked, not unreasonably.

# Miracle Run

Zac was widely acclaimed by critics and reviewers for his portrayal of Steven Morgan, one of a pair of autistic twins, in *Miracle Run*, a 2004 film directed by Gregg Champion. In some countries it was released with the alternative title *The Unexpected Journey*. 'I was so happy to get that role,' he told *Life Story* magazine. 'I got the call and they asked me to do the movie. Within the next day or two, I flew out and began shooting in Louisiana and it was amazing.' The film also starred Mary-Louise Parker and Aidan Quinn as his parents, and Thomas 'Bubba' Lewis played his brother. This was Zac's first really meaty dramatic part, and he made sure that he read up on autism so

that he had the necessary background knowledge for the role. He wanted to make sure that he gave an accurate portrayal of the condition, and he has said that he found Temple Grandin's book *Thinking in Pictures: My Life with Autism* particularly helpful. 'After a few chapters, I was more educated by far than the average person on autism,' he said.

Aidan Quinn, whose daughter has autism, paid tribute to how well Zac and Bubba did in portraying the condition: 'I was kind of amazed at the job they did,' Quinn told a newspaper. 'In a short period of time, they learned certain looks, ways of walking and holding their hands – things that are particular to autistic kids that, when you're the parent of an autistic child, you know inside and out.' The critics agreed with Aidan's positive assessment of their performances, and Zac was nominated for a Young Artist Award for Best Supporting Actor. *Variety* was also very impressed by the portrayal of the young twins, saying that Zac and Bubba were 'commendable in their performances for not resorting to stereotypes of the developmentally disabled.' Not a bad write up for a young actor in his first big role.

# Modesty

Although Zac is one of Hollywood's rising stars, he's careful not to let it go to his head, and he's unfailingly modest about his success. 'I could show you 500 kids in LA who are my height, weight, hair colour and age,' he told the *Toronto Star* in 2007. 'We're a dime a dozen. Why did I get the parts I did? Who knows? But the minute I start thinking it's because I was special, that's when I know I'm in trouble.'

Obviously, there must be something special about Zac – there wouldn't be co-stars falling over themselves to praise him and directors keen to work with him otherwise. But this refusal to let things go to his head is a refreshing perspective when you consider how successful and popular Zac is, and contrast it with the diva-like behaviour that's often reported concerning other stars. But he hopes his success encourages other kids to follow their dream, saying, 'Hey, if it happened to me, then, man, it can happen to anybody.'

# Music

Zac has a very eclectic taste in music, and enjoys going to concerts with friends and family. Although his parents weren't musical, they liked music so he grew up listening to it a lot. He says that he'll listen to any style of music 'from Joy Division to early

ZAC IS SAID TO BE A MASSIVE KINGS OF LEON FAN.

reggae,' as he puts it – well, anything except country music, that is! He also likes British groups Radiohead, Kasabian and Coldplay, and an American band called The Postal Service, who got their name because they collaborated on tracks by sending tapes to each other through the mail. Zac says that Kings of Leon do a great live show – he got the chance to catch them when he was in Australia in 2009. He was also pretty gutted that he had to miss the Yeah Yeah Yeahs when they performed on *Saturday Night Live*. He was invited to their show but had to be up early for work so couldn't go.

If that's not specific enough for you, when Zac was asked for five songs that everyone should have on their iPod, he chose 'You Are Not Alone' by Michael Jackson, 'Weapon of Choice' by Fat Boy Slim, 'Chasing Cars' by Snow Patrol, 'Boston' by Augustana, and 'Digital Love' by Daft Punk. So, now you know!

# Musicals

Even though Zac has taken a break from performing in musicals for a while – mainly because he didn't want to be typecast after making his name in *High*

*School Musical* and *Hairspray* – he still loves the musical genre. He started out in musical theatre and clearly enjoyed every minute – and learned a lot in the process. 'I feel like it's a whole different skill set you get to prepare for a film,' he said during the making of *Hairspray*. 'Like doing theatre and that's where I fell in love with entertaining, in musical theatre.' He has huge admiration for stars like Hugh Jackman who manage to combine serious acting with first-class musical and dance ability.

As well as appearing in musicals as a child, Zac watched a lot of musical films. His favourite is, by far, *Singing In The Rain*. He says that he has watched it dozens of times. 'Gene Kelly is a master performer and he's got a sense of charisma I aspire to possess one day,' he says. He first saw the film at a key point in his life and it made a real impression: 'I must have been 14 when I first saw it. I was getting into performing as a hobby and I really looked up to his performance in that film,' says Zac.

So, it seems that although Zac has moved away from musicals in the short term, so he can establish himself as a more mainstream actor, he hasn't ruled out returning to the genre at some point in the future. He says that he is keen to take a role on Broadway at some point in the future – maybe this is when he'll get back into the musical theatre that started him off?

# Music videos

Although Zac didn't want to take the opportunity of a musical career off the back of *High School Musical*, his girlfriend Vanessa did, and released a number of records. Zac was happy to support her, taking a role as her boyfriend in the video for her single 'Say OK', which was released in 2007. The video was directed by Darren Grant and was filmed in a bowling alley and on a beach in Los Angeles. It got nearly 90 million views when it was put on YouTube! It might be tempting to wonder whether all of these were because of the song…

# N is for...

## Nicknames

Zac sometimes goes by the nickname 'Zefron' – and this is the name of the fansite most closely associated with him. His friends from his home town nicknamed him 'Hollywood' when he started making films, and it seems to have stuck. He's also sometimes referred to as 'Zacquisha,' a nickname coined by the often cruel celebrity blogger Perez Hilton. Perez dismisses Zac as a 'pretty boy' and once accused him of wearing false eyelashes! Zac

FRIENDS FROM
HIS HOMETOWN
HAVE NICKNAMED
ZAC 'HOLLYWOOD'.

told *GQ* magazine that he has never worn false eyelashes, and 'if somebody can find any photo that shows me wearing false eyelashes,' he says, 'I will give them a million dollars.' So, we won't call you Zacquisha then, Zac?

# Nikki Blonsky

Nikki Blonsky played Tracy Turnblad, the plump dance fanatic in the film *Hairspray*. Her character is the one who finally ends up with Zac's character, Link Larkin. It was Nikki's first film role, and Zac says he was prepared to take her under his wing a bit. 'I was, compared to Nikki, slightly more experienced with the limited work I've done. I was kind of prepared to be helping her and encouraging her and maybe possibly teaching her something,' he said. But as it turned out, it wasn't like that at all. Zac found that he was watching Nikki instead, and was blown away by her talent and her approach to her work. 'I found myself taking tips from Nikki. She was so brilliant in everything she does. She tries everything. She is so courageous. So talented, you can say she's never done anything before, but it's

almost not right. She's been ready for this moment her whole life,' he said.

It's clear that they got on brilliantly on a personal level too – Zac said that, 'there's no one better to work with. We honestly became best friends,' and he also said on a TV show that he thought that he and Nikki had 'a thing' – and the two actors were badgered into reprising their screen kiss! Nikki was clearly as fond of Zac as he was of her and said, 'I love him with every inch of my body and soul. He has been an amazing support system.' Cute!

Opposite: Zac's *Hairspray* co-star, Nikki Blonsky.

# O is for...

## Oscars

Zac may still be waiting for his first Academy Award nomination, but he's already had a taste of the Oscar magic. For the 2010 awards, Zac was invited to join the list of stars who presented the awards. Together with Anna Kendrick, he presented the awards for Best Sound Mixing and Best Sound Editing. Was he nervous about getting up and making a speech in front of millions of viewers all over the world? Well, yes, he was a bit! But, he said, it had its up-side as

ZAC ATTENDS THE
OSCARS IN 2010.

well: 'I kind of thrive on it. Part of growing up onstage is that you feel alive at these things.'

Zac was clearly excited to be part of the whole Oscars phenomenon, and on the red carpet he said that he was blown away from seeing the most inspiring actors and directors all around him. He said that directors James Cameron and Quentin Tarantino were among the people he was excited to see, and reportedly turned a bit star struck when he bumped into *Avatar's* Sam Worthington. 'I saw it [*Avatar*] four times; I've seen you [Worthington] in 3D, regular, HD – I've seen you in every "D" possible... You are the man, dude. It's great to see you,' he said to his fellow actor.

# P is for...

## Parents

Unlike a lot of his contemporaries in the acting world, Zac didn't come from a showbiz family with the stereotypical pushy parents – far from it. He says he 'lived a normal childhood in a middle-class family' and that when he was growing up he certainly had no idea of going into the movies one day: 'When I was younger, I didn't even know this business existed,' he said. He now says that his family think the whole Zac-phenomenon is really strange.

ZAC AND HIS MOTHER STARLA ARE MOBBED BY PAPARAZZI AS THEY LEAVE
THE AIRPORT.

'My family think it's hilarious,' he told Australian journalist, Mel Doyle.

Zac's parents were really proud of him from the beginning. He was, according to them at least, pretty cute from the start. His dad, David, said that he looked just like the babies who appeared on baby food commercials! He was a friendly baby too – 'he cried if you left him alone, and he loved to be held,' added Zac's dad in an interview with America's *J-14* magazine.

Zac's dad, whom Zac describes as someone who 'operates from the left hemisphere, very logical,' is an engineer and he met Zac's mum, Starla, at work – she was working at the same power plant as a secretary at the time. Zac says that his mum is 'a hippie in the best way possible, very spiritual'. But it was his dad who sensed that Zac might have some talent in singing and acting and encouraged him to take roles in musicals – including lining up his first audition.

Zac's parents are very proud of what their son has achieved, but they're clearly a pretty big part of the reason that so many people talk about how 'normal' and 'grounded' Zac is. He recently told *GQ* magazine that his parents 'give it to you real. I didn't grow up thinking I was the greatest kid in the world.' Although they have clearly supported Zac as he has followed his dreams to be an actor, encouraging him at every turn and taking him to audition after audition, 'they completely believed that there was a one-in-a-billion chance I would ever be successful. And that was ingrained in the back of my head… I was always prepared to fail. So it was kind of confusing when things started to work out.' This was probably why they insisted that he keep up with his education and study hard at school – if the movie business hadn't worked out, Zac would have had his straight 'A's' and a place at university to fall back on.

Zac says that when he was growing up, his parents kept a pretty close eye on him – he didn't get away with much and there were no wild parties at his house – he even had trouble going to other people's parties! He says that he never thought he'd be grateful for such a strict upbringing, but he now says that he's really thankful for the way his mum and dad raised him. 'I credit my family 100 per cent,' Zac says 'They taught me everything. My parents are the smartest people I know.' There was a rumour that Zac had wanted to express his gratitude to his mother by having her name tattooed on his arm – but, we're told, he dropped the idea when she said she didn't want him to!

# Pets

Zac has some much-loved pets. He has a Siamese cat called Simon, and two Australian Shepherd dogs, called Dreamer and Puppy. The dogs are clearly much loved members of Zac's family, if slightly mischievous ones. 'My dogs are crazy,' Zac says. 'They're always getting into some kind of trouble … but then again, they're my most loyal friends.' Dreamer was his first pet and a few years ago, she had a bit of a weight problem, which meant that she struggled to keep up on their daily runs. 'We put her on a diet. Now she's back to normal,' says Zac. And once Dreamer was her former svelte self, Zac tried to teach her new tricks – but it seems that the saying about old dogs and new tricks has some truth to it. 'I'm trying to teach her to catch a Frisbee,' he says, 'but it doesn't seem to always work.'

# Premières

Zac attends a lot of premières for his films, and has got quite used to the pandemonium, paparazzi and red carpet interviews that inevitably form part of

ZAC AT THE PREMIÈRE
OF *17 AGAIN*.

the première experience. He enjoys seeing his fans and is always appreciative of their support for him and his film projects. But there have been times when it has all got a bit out of hand. He describes one of his premières in Mexico as the craziest he's attended: 'It was just chaos. We couldn't enter from the front of the theatre. I remember security was going nuts, and everyone was freaking out and running around. We actually had to sneak in to our own première through a back entrance and walk all the way through the theatre to the front. There were so many people out in the streets that we couldn't go out. It was pandemonium.'

Zac is even left with unwelcome souvenirs from premières from time to time. 'I was at a première and there was a huge crowd that got completely out of control,' he told the *Daily Mail*. 'A barrier broke and fans came rushing over and grabbed me. I was pulled in every direction. The security guards stopped the commotion and no one was hurt, but later that night I went home, took off my shirt and was getting ready for bed when I found a long fingernail stuck into my back.' Ewww!

Zac says that the noise that fans make can be deafening, especially if he's indoors. He says that he doesn't understand how girls manage to make the particular noise they make – 'I don't understand how that comes out!' he says. He admits that there is sometimes a temptation to avoid the noise because he worries about his hearing. 'It does get to the point where it's unhealthy. You can't walk the carpet, and nobody can do an interview.' This means that sometimes his red carpet interviews aren't as meaningful as they could be. 'I can't hear anything! So I end up looking in the camera and nodding,' he says. 'Whatever they ask, I'll be like, "Yeah, it's great to be here! I'm so excited about the movie!"'

# Preparation

Zac is pretty scrupulous about making sure he's well prepared for the roles he takes on. Kenny Ortega has talked a lot about how hard Zac worked on the choreography and the basketball skills he needed for the *High School Musical* films, but it seems that Zac does a huge amount of preparation work for every role he takes. He read up on autism before his appearance in *Miracle Run*, prepared for his role in *Me and Orson Welles* by studying the iconic director and watching his films, and spent ages studying Matthew Perry's mannerisms to play his younger self in *17 Again*.

Brian Michael Bendis, who approached Zac to work on *Fire*, said that Zac was keen to do all the prep work necessary for that film too: 'I'll tell you, I hit him with a list of books and movies that I thought would be appropriate for him to get into for this spy genre. Literally the next time I saw him he had already gotten through half the list,' he said. 'And I really liked that – I'd like that about anybody. It showed he was serious, so I was digging it.'

# Privacy

Zac is always happy to stop and say hello to fans, and sees giving interviews about his projects as part of his job – and a part that he wants to do well. But he is famously cagey about his private life. He has frequently said that he doesn't want to be famous for his personality – if he's going to be well known, he wants it to be for the work he does, not what he thinks or who he dates. Zac and Vanessa were a couple for a long time before they went public with their relationship. Even on the set of *High School Musical 2*, one member of the crew said that they were already really good at keeping their cards close to their chests. 'If you didn't know they were dating, you wouldn't know they were dating,' the crew member said. 'They're really good at not being obvious.'

Although Zac loves his work, he has said that he finds a lot of the trappings of fame 'pretty un-adorable'. He admits to taking steps to avoid photographers – some of his friends have said that meeting up with him can be quite a surreal experience because of the chasing about they have to do to avoid paparazzi. Similarly, he's not willing to discuss his politics, either. He very happily got involved in a campaign to encourage young people to register to vote but wouldn't publicly endorse a candidate. He's very wary of what he has called the 'internet pandemonium' that results from all the rumours, so he does his best not to feed them.

OPPOSITE: ZAC ENJOYS MEETING HIS FANS BUT ALSO LIKES TO KEEP HIS PRIVATE LIFE PRIVATE.

# Punk'd

*Punk'd* was an American TV show, which was broadcast on MTV. It used hidden cameras and played practical jokes on well known people – usually with the assistance of their friends – and was produced and hosted by Ashton Kutcher. On the show, being 'punk'd' referred to being the victim of such a prank.

Zac's *High School Musical* co-star Ashley Tisdale was the accomplice for the show when Zac was 'punk'd' in 2007. The prank was set up at a clothes store and when the sales assistant leaves to pop to another shop and the security guard vanishes, two guys walk in and take the cash box. Eventually, the security guard brings in one of them and Zac confirms he's the right guy – but then the other man, the one who actually took the box, comes in and Zac is told he's an employee who was off work. The owner gets mad at Zac for accusing the wrong guy, voices are raised, accusations fly… and then the hidden camera is revealed. Zac took the joke very well – but given his reputation as a practical joker on the set of *High School Musical*, he probably didn't have much choice about that!

# Q is for...

## Quentin Tarantino

Zac is a big fan of Quentin Tarantino, and loves his gritty films like *Pulp Fiction* and *Reservoir Dogs*. He has mentioned *Pulp Fiction* as an example of the kind of film he'd like to make at some point in the future – although he says he knows that he's got a bit of work to do before he's ready to take on something so hard-hitting. He name-checked Tarantino at the 2010 Oscars as being an iconic director whom he would love to work with in the future. And who knows, it

could be sooner than he thinks! Tarantino says that he isn't just about the hard and gritty – he has said he'd love to tell a love story, and he's actually a big fan of romantic comedies. 'These rom-coms get a bad rap but actually I'm a fan of romantic comedies – they usually work on wordplay and everything like that, so I actually think I'd be really good at it,' he said. And Zac's set to perform in a grittier role in his new project, *Easy Money*. So, Zac, you never know, you might be meeting Quentin halfway...

OPPOSITE: FILM DIRECTOR QUENTIN TARANTINO.

# R is for...

## Richard Linklater

Richard Linklater, who had previously made hit films like *Dazed and Confused* and *Before Sunrise*, directed Zac in *Me and Orson Welles*, and the two clearly had a great working relationship and an enormous amount of respect for each other. Linklater says that Zac had been his first choice for the part of Richard after he'd seen him in *Hairspray*. He says that he thought Zac was really smart and worked hard, and had real 'leading man qualities' of charisma and screen presence.

Zac had a great relationship with *Me and Orson Welles* director Richard Linklater.

Zac was thrilled to be asked to consider a part in one of Richard's films, as he was a big fan of his work, and had seen lots of his previous movies. He says that he was 'floored' when he heard that Linklater wanted to meet him.

Richard was really impressed by the way Zac stepped up to the challenge in the film: 'Here he is, this kid from California stepping into a group of accomplished British actors, and he was so not intimidated.' Richard also says that people who dismiss Zac as being a squeaky-clean Disney kid are really missing a trick. 'I would never take Zac at face value,' he says. 'He's actually a bit of a poker player. He comes in all nice and then he just takes your money. I think you underestimate Zac at your own peril.' That'll be the streak of determination Zac's dad was talking about, then!

So this is another director who clearly sees that Zac has the potential to transcend his teen-musical background and move on to bigger and better things.

Zac's admiration for Richard Linklater seems to have deepened further after the two worked together, saying that the director's philosophy is inspiring, and that watching the process he goes through to make a film was amazing. 'If there's a way,' Zac says, 'he will find it.'

# Rings

There was widespread speculation a few years back when Zac was seen wearing a silver 'commitment' ring, but at the time he refused to talk about what it signified, or even say who gave it to him. 'I'm not even going to say who it's from. This is just a ring from a friend that I got… It is a female friend, but I can't say who, because then it would be chat-room pandemonium and teenage magazine hysteria,' he said, cagily.

But Zac was mistaken if he thought that keeping quiet would stop the gossip. The gossip and 'chat-room pandemonium' continued despite Zac's silence on the matter – and when his relationship with Vanessa finally went public, most fans assumed that the mystery – such as it was – had been solved.

# Robert Pattinson

Zac and Robert Pattinson are the two hottest male stars around, so despite the fact that they frequently chat happily to each other at events, and are clearly on friendly terms, there is a continuous stream of gossip as people speculate that they are secretly rivals. The logic, such as it is, is that they're both young, good-looking and successful – so they must absolutely hate each other, right?

It's true that Zac said that he liked Robert being on the scene because it took away some of the pressure of female attention – and some people took that as being a jibe at the *Twilight* star. But rumours earlier this year, that Zac was jealous of the attention Rob had got at the MTV awards, and that Zac thought Rob 'looked like a homeless person,' were dismissed as pure fantasy. Zac said that he really thought Robert was amazing. 'I think he's making great choices. I think he's handling it all really well, but you know, he's a superstar. He really deserves all this,' he said. Robert told *OK!* Magazine that Zac was a really cool guy and described the first time they met as being 'one of the first times I'd ever been star struck.'

So, if there's a rivalry, it's not being played out in public, that's for certain. Unlike the gossip columnists, both Zac and Rob are too professional for that.

*TWILIGHT* STAR ROBERT PATTINSON.

# Rumoured projects

There were rumours about a film starring Zac with a working title of 'Algorithm' and it was announced this year that it's now to be called *Einstein Theory* and is set for release in 2012. Details are very thin on the ground because the film isn't yet in production, but sources report that it'll be a modern take on the ideas behind the 1980s hit *Back to the Future* movies, and it's been confirmed by the studio that Zac is currently involved.

It has also been reported that Zac has signed up to take part in *Fire*, an adaptation of a graphic novel by Brian Michael Bendis. Zac is well known as being a big comic fan, so this could be right up his street. The plan is, apparently, for Zac to play a college student who is recruited by the CIA, only to find that he has been trained for a program that creates expendable agents. Bendis met up with Zac to discuss the film and he said that Zac was interesting and very smart and 'trying to make that next step in a legitimate way.' He was impressed that Zac was clearly knowledgeable about the project and a fan of the original novel. 'He's a fan all the way. He talked about it in great detail, what he liked about it and what he wanted from it,' he said.

There are also rumours that Zac is lined up to take a role in a film based on the story of Christian the lion, which was a sensation on YouTube, with more than 100 million hits all over the world. Zac is, apparently, in the frame to play John Rendall, who raised a lion cub and then released him into the wild. There has been no confirmation of this so we should probably not hold our breath for Zac doing any lion-cub cuddling very soon.

# S is for...

## Saturday Night Live

Although Zac does love acting, he also gets a kick out of presenting, possibly because it takes him back to his days starting out in live theatre. And one of the things he found really exciting was being invited to host *Saturday Night Live*, a well respected sketch comedy show, broadcast on the NBC network. 'I'm so excited to host SNL,' Zac enthused, 'It's been a dream of mine since I was 10 years old. Improv is pretty much how I got started. They do more sketch comedy, but, yeah, this is how I started. This is what I want to get back to. I think it's going to be a great week. I can't wait.'

Zac got some good reviews on his performance as host: *Entertainment Weekly*'s critic said he was pleasant and up for just about anything. He got some laughs with his opening monologue in which he played on his having a young fan base by saying, 'For those of you who don't know me, my name is Zac Efron... For those of you who do know me... thanks for staying up so late!' Zac was widely applauded for taking part in lots of comedy sketches – including one where his comedian co-star tried to suck his toes! – and for being willing to have a go at anything. Among the sketches in the show was a *High School Musical* parody, in which Troy returns to East High to break it to students that no singing is allowed at college, and that on his first day he felt nervous and excited. 'So I started singing a song called "Nervous But Excited". People just stared at me! There was zero choreography!' This light-hearted reference to Zac's best known role went down especially well with viewers and critics.

Zac clearly felt honoured to be asked to host *Saturday Night Live* and described the experience as a life-changing week, saying that putting the show together had been 'really gruelling but a lot of fun.'

# 17 Again

*17 Again* is a quirky feel-good movie that was released in 2009, and stars both Zac and Matthew Perry as Mike O'Donnell. How come they both play the same role? Well, Mike, as played by Matthew, is 37 and fed up with how his life has turned out. He's lost his job, his wife Scarlett (played by Leslie Mann) has left him, and their two kids, Maggie (Michelle Trachtenberg) and Alex (Sterling Knight), want to have nothing to do with him. But an encounter with a mysterious caretaker at his old high school transforms the hapless Mike back into his 17-year-old self – who's played by Zac!

In the guise of his younger self, Mike enlists the help of his best friend Ned, and posing as Ned's fictional son Mark, he returns to high school so he can keep a close eye on his children. And, of course, in the process he becomes the coolest guy in school. It's not all plain sailing – Mike finds himself having to fend off the advances of both his estranged wife (who is, of course, old enough to be his mother) and his daughter. Despite the potential for confusion, Zac jumped at the role. 'It was exactly what I was looking for,' he said. 'This was an opportunity to

Zac's *17 Again* co-star, Michelle Trachtenberg.

work with a brilliant cast and an amazing director. And, yeah, it was a chance to switch it up. It does take place in a high school setting, but it's not a very high school character, so that's what I want to do more of.'

Playing a 37-year-old man in a 17-year-old's body was not without its challenges, though. Zac found that he had no direct experience to draw on, so it was hard to prepare. 'I've never had a daughter who I'm looking out for. I've never been proud of my son. I've never gotten a divorce. It was interesting trying to figure that out. It was definitely a change of pace,' he said. Zac suspects that Burr Steers, the director, sometimes found it frustrating to direct him as he worked on the role because it was hard to find points of common experience to draw on. 'It would be so easy for him to see where a father would come from in a situation, and he would try to communicate that to me. Inevitably, he would realise there were so few ways I could relate to a 37-year-old guy! That was interesting,' he told *Buzzine*. But he said that the director did help him find his feet in the role. 'He's got this huge imagination, and this sense of people – not what they seem to be, or what they're defined to be, or what they want to appear to be, but as they actually are,' said Zac.

Zac feels that the role was a natural step on from his role in the *High School Musical* films. 'A lot of stuff I had done until now I've lived. First love – been there, done that. High school. Putting on plays. In *Hairspray*… well, that's a little different! Well, still the same kind of thing. I've done that, I've experienced it,' he explained. 'Whereas in this movie, I'm doing things that someone twice my age has barely done yet.' Which can only be a good thing, as it prepared him for the next step in his career.

The film did really well, making $135 million and ending its opening weekend at number one. Zac won two Teen Choice awards for his part in the movie, for Movie Actor: Comedy and Rockstar Moment, as well as a nomination for Best Male Performance at the MTV Movie awards. It also got some good reviews, with the *Daily Mail* describing it as 'canny as well as cute' and praising Zac's talent for light comedy. *Film 4* said that the film succeeded in turning Zac 'from a long-lashed cutesy baby into something more, well, interesting.'

# Singing

Zac's focus has been on acting for a while, but it was his talent for singing that was noticed first. Apparently, Zac didn't exactly come from a family of songbirds: 'When I was younger, my dad noticed that whatever song came on the radio, I would sing along with it, and that I could carry a tune, which was different to anyone in our family.' His parents, although not singers themselves, both love music, and when they realised that their son had a good voice, they encouraged him to make use of it. His dad took him for an audition for a part in a musical, which he got, and then it went from there.

It's not at all surprising that after the success of the *High School Musical* films and *Hairspray*, there was a lot of interest in Zac as a singer. He says that there were lots of people who wanted him to sing again, and lots of singing opportunities suggested to him. He was even approached by *American Idol* judge Simon Cowell – who didn't come straight out with an offer of a record deal, but instead, according to Zac, 'he was simply asking if I wanted to pursue that because if I did, he wanted to work with me.'

But Zac turned down this offer, and all the offers

to make records, because he wanted to concentrate on his acting. 'I didn't want to do what everyone else did,' he told *Entertainment Weekly*. 'I thought to myself, "What can I contribute to the music industry?" I can't say that I would be proud of the work I would put down.'

As much as he enjoys music, and although it's clear from everything that he has said that he has loved working on the musicals he has done, Zac is definitely focused more on his acting than his singing. He says, 'I like to sing, but I'm not looking for a record label or anything.' He has also made it very clear that even if he does make a record one day, he has no interest in being a pre-packaged pop star singing formulaic songs that someone else has written. If he goes into a studio, it will be to record music that he's written himself. 'I think the day I could make an album is the day I could write and produce it on my own terms and when I have the skills and wisdom to do it,' he says. Zac is clearly keen to keep control of what he does and not get caught up in fame for its own sake, which ties in with his well-documented work ethic.

# Smoking

As you'd expect from someone who takes such good care of his health and fitness, Zac has never smoked and he says he never intends to. He is quite vocal about his dislike of smoking, too. He said in one interview that cigarettes are his pet peeve and he hates being around smokers or even smelling cigarette smoke, and in another interview he said that smoking is one of the things a girl could do that would stop a potential relationship in its tracks. 'Smoking would be the thing that would make an impossible match for me,' he told *People* magazine.

# Snabba Cash

The internet went mad in early 2010 when it was reported that Zac was going to be involved in a new project called *Snabba Cash* – a film which is certainly set to shatter anything that remains of his squeaky-clean Disney image into a million pieces.

The project is an English-language remake of the 2006 Swedish film *Snabba Cash* which was directed by Daniel Espinosa, and based on the book by Jens Lapidus. It was a hit in Sweden, and a cult success elsewhere. 'Snabba Cash' translates roughly as 'fast cash' or 'easy money' and *Easy Money* is probably going to be the name of the film when it's released. The plot centres on drugs and organised crime, and follows the story of a young man from the country who becomes a runner for a notorious drug dealer in order to make some fast money. There's some speculation that the US adaptation would involve money laundering rather than drugs. So, all in all, a bit of a departure from *High School Musical* and *Hairspray*!

It sounds as though Zac was really keen to be involved, but he had to lobby pretty hard to convince the producer, Fredrik Wilkström, that he had what it takes. 'I was a bit sceptical of Zac from the start, given what he has been in in the past, such as the *High School Musical* movies,' said Wikström. This is probably why Zac feels that the musicals he has done, although they gave him his big break, might sometimes hold him back a bit, and why he has been so determined to get new experiences and broaden his talents whenever he can. But it seems that he managed to win the producer round. 'But after meeting him,' said Wikström, 'I am completely convinced. He's very good… He has been offered a lot of action [roles] but this is what he wants to do… He's perfect for the part, and he seemed very committed to the assignment.'

The US rights were subject to a bidding war, but Warner Brothers, with Zac's involvement, won out in the end. Zac is expected to co-produce the movie, as well as take one of the lead roles. Some critics have said that Zac risks alienating his fans by taking on more adult subjects, but then again, Zac's fans are getting older at the same rate as he is. Perhaps moving away from the Disney image is a shrewd move for him?

# Sports

It comes as no surprise to learn that Zac is really into sports, both as a participant and as a spectator. He supports the San Francisco Giants baseball team, describing himself as a huge fan. He's very proud of his collection of signed baseballs – he has managed to get hold of one from nearly every Giants player from the past decade! – and described them as his most treasured possession.

Zac is a fan of adrenaline sports, particularly surfing. He loves the beach – especially in Australia, where he can find great beaches that are all but deserted. He admits that despite his enthusiasm, he's not a brilliant surfer: 'For the first week of surfing every single wave hits you head-on. It seems like they're never going to stop and you're getting ripped to pieces by these waves.' But as in so many areas, Zac is prepared to persevere. 'That first moment when you actually jump up and you're on the open face of a wave is amazing. All the energy was going against you and now you've mastered it.'

He also enjoys basketball, which he learned to play well for his roles in *High School Musical* and *Hairspray*, and supports the LA Lakers. He says, 'I wanted to be a player when I was younger [but] I was too small. I've always been a small kid.' He didn't do particularly well playing basketball as a child – 'I think I scored two points my entire basketball season,' he admits – but that didn't diminish his love for the game. Although it turned out not to be a viable career option, Zac still enjoys playing basketball, and enjoyed the opportunity to improve his skills and his game that came with the *High School Musical* movies and then *Hairspray*. He takes part in basketball games for fun whenever he gets the chance. He's also famously keen on keeping fit, starting his day with a run whenever he can – even if it means going out before dawn – and going to the gym five days a week. It's no wonder he's in such good shape!

ZAC GREETS HIS ADORING FANS DURING A PREMIÈRE.

# Sterling Knight

Zac and his *17 Again* co-star Sterling Knight may get on well these days, but their first meeting wasn't that auspicious. Sterling told US talk-show host Bonnie Hunt that for a while his feelings towards Zac weren't friendly at all, because Zac was turning out to be tough competition. 'I had auditioned for *High School Musical* and this movie, *The Derby Stallion*, that he had done, and I was really frustrated,' Sterling explained. 'This kid, Zac Efron – curse him! – is booking everything I'm auditioning for!' We can probably understand that being up against Zac for role after role must have been incredibly frustrating!

To make matters worse, one day, when he was on his way to play golf, Sterling found himself blocked in by a film crew. He saw red and totally lost his temper with one of the actors – who, as luck would have it, turned out to be Zac, of course! Oh dear… A year later the two met once more on the set of *17 Again*, and Sterling reminded Zac of their previous meeting and confessed that he had been the bad tempered driver who had subjected him to the tirade. Thankfully, Zac was happy to let bygones be bygones and Sterling says that the two of them now get along fine!

# Summerland

*Summerland* was a TV show created by Lori Loughlin, an actress who'd had a massive hit in the 1990s with *Full House* – the series that had brought Mary-Kate and Ashley Olsen to the public eye. *Summerland* was a drama, set in a coastal community in California – a setting which Zac would be very familiar with as it was similar to the town where he'd grown up.

Loughlin herself played Ava, an ambitious and career-driven fashion designer who has to reassess her priorities when her sister and brother-in-law are killed and Ava is left with their three children. *Summerland* aired in the summer of 2004, and although it didn't make huge waves in the ratings, it quickly gathered a cult following. The story of the three children being raised by their somewhat eccentric aunt wasn't a fluffy teen drama and it didn't shy away from the important issues surrounding adolescence, bereavement and family dynamics. Eventually, the producers decided that they needed to inject fresh blood into the show to keep it fresh. Enter the role of Cameron Bale, a good-looking 14-year-old with his fair share of demons. Zac campaigned to wangle an audition, got it and

ZAC'S SUMMERLAND CO-STAR KAY PANABAKER.

obviously nailed it, because they gave him the role after that single audition.

Initially, the character of Cameron was written into the show for a couple of episodes in Season One, but Zac did so well, and fitted in to the cast so perfectly, that they decided to keep him on as a full cast member in the second season. This was Zac's big break, a regular cast appearance in a popular TV show. He kicked off his filming on the show by kissing his co-star, Kay Panabaker. 'The first scene I ever did on *Summerland* was a make-out scene with Kay. Those are really tough, but everyone made me feel right at home. It made me feel like part of the cast,' he said.

It was during the filming of *Summerland* that Zac first met Taylor Lautner. Taylor is most often bracketed together with Robert Pattinson because they appeared in the Twilight films together, but back in 2003 Taylor landed a small part in an episode of *Summerland*. Who would have predicted that a show with a cult following and which only managed a short run would end up giving Hollywood not one, but two big stars?

As well as being his big break, *Summerland* gave Zac an insight into the realities of acting. 'I got to build a family with the people at *Summerland*. I would see them three days a week, and I got to feel what it was like and test the waters.'

The second season of *Summerland* ended on a high note, and Zac was really excited about the developments and the gritty storylines that were set for Cameron in the next season. Unfortunately, it was not to be. The network cancelled the show in 2005. That was the end of Zac's big break, and his hopes of developing Cameron into a really serious character. Nonetheless, Zac had made his mark, both with directors and with fans – it was during the run of *Summerland* that Zac's first fan site got up and running.

# Superheroes

Zac is a comic fan, so it's not surprising that he'd like to take on a superhero role in the future. When Tobey Maguire announced that he would not be making any further *Spider-man* movies, speculation over who would take his place ran riot – and Zac was considered to be in the frame. While he was realistic about the chances of him securing the role, there was no doubt that he was keen. 'I don't know what the chances are, to be honest. I assume they're pretty slim,' he said, when asked by the press about the possibility of him taking the role. 'It's a long shot

ANDREW GARFIELD WILL BE PLAYING SPIDER-MAN IN THE REBOOT OF THE SUPERHERO SAGA.

but if it came down to it, it'd be a dream come true. What young actor wouldn't?' Especially a young actor who has apparently loved Spider-man comics since he was six...

The rumour mill surrounding the film intensified, and by early 2010 *Empire* magazine named Zac as the 'rumoured studio frontrunner' to play Spider-man. But sadly, it was not to be − in June 2010 it was reported that Andrew Garfield had been cast instead. But there's plenty of time yet for Zac to land a superhero role − oh, and the tights, of course...

# T is for...

## Theatre

Zac does the majority of his work on the big screen now, but he still has a lot of time for the theatre, where he started out. He spent most of his childhood in plays and musicals in local theatres, and says that this experience is what got him enthusiastic about acting. 'The way you catch the bug and fall in love with this business is to do theatre. It's so nice to be in front of an audience and feel their energy. It really sparks your passion,' he told the American magazine,

*Teen Dream*. He has alluded to the fact that his formative experience in the theatre means that he still gets a buzz from being in front of a large audience – which is why he got such a kick from presenting at the 2010 Oscars, and audiences don't get much bigger than that!

It's been a long time since Zac has acted on stage rather than on screen, and there are always rumours flying about that he's going to be in this Broadway show or that West End play. So far, these rumours haven't come to anything, but Zac has said that he'd like to do more stage work in the future. In an interview in June 2010, he said that every time he was on Broadway he wanted to go back to live theatre. 'Every time I see a show on Broadway I get this deep-seated feeling that I want to be up on stage with those guys,' he said. But sadly, Zac can't fit the demands of theatre into a busy schedule. 'It would be such a challenge getting the time away to do it. But if I could I would, and I hope I can soon,' he added.

He also says that for anyone who wants to get into acting, the theatre is the place to start. 'There's no better way to learn skills,' he says. 'Go out and try theatre. Local theatre is everywhere.'

A YOUTHFUL LOOKING ZAC DURING A LIVE PERFORMANCE OF *HAIRSPRAY*.

# Teeth

Zac's perfect teeth have been another cause for speculation. Some people have even wondered if they are really his own teeth, which led Zac to lose his patience a bit and retort that they could hardly belong to someone else! Zac did once have a gap between his front teeth, but it was fixed by a short stint with invisible braces. 'The gap was actually very small,' he said. 'When I went on camera, especially on TV, it would distort it and make it look really big.' He says that he's happy with the way his teeth look now!

# Travel

Zac loves to travel, and finds it a great way of escaping the pressures he has to deal with at home in Los Angeles. He says that he's at his happiest when he's away from home, not just because he can get around with less attention, but because he can find new things. 'I love finding interesting things in culture. I love travelling to new places,' he told *Buzzine*. 'Anywhere where I'm not sitting down and I feel like I'm growing

Zac meets his adoring fans at the London première of *Me & Orson Welles.*

Our favourite actor signs autographs at LAX airport.

*Above*: Zac and co-star Amanda Crew at the première of *Charlie St. Cloud*.

*Below*: Zac has a close relationship with his mother, Starla, who has supported him throughout his career.

*Left*: Since finishing the final *High School Musical* film, Zac has been looking for more advanced roles to develop his budding career.

*Above*: Vanessa and Zac are spotted out and about in LA.

Zac played Link Larkin in the hit movie *Hairspray*.

*Above*: Vanessa and Zac at the Oscars in 2009.

*Left*: Zac takes a break from filming *Me & Orson Welles*.

*Left*: Zac posing with his "Best Breakthrough Performance" award at the 2008 MTV Movie Awards.

*Right*: A waxwork version of Zac can be seen at Madame Tussauds in Times Square, New York.

or learning or improving myself, then I'm pretty happy.' He gets to travel a fair bit with work, and he definitely does his best to make the most of those opportunities. He has said that he really enjoys visiting Australia, because it's relaxed – and there's so much space that he can sometimes manage to find a beach all to himself! 'I've always had an affinity towards the ocean and towards a beach lifestyle, and no place does that better than Australia,' he says. 'Actually, this is one of the few places where I can surf these days...' He has also spent a fair bit of time in the UK, and says that he always enjoys being on our side of the Atlantic. He also loves Hawaii, describing it as 'the kind of place you could come and never leave.' He says that he's attracted to Hawaii by the surfing, the jungle and the friendly people. He told interviewers at the Maui Film Festival that Hawaii was one of the few places in the world where he felt he had a reason to get up at 7 a.m.!

## Troy Bolton

Playing Troy Bolton in the first three *High School Musical* films was how Zac went from rising star to *bona fide* superstar. As one of East High's most popular

THE ORIGINAL CAST
of *High School
Musical* POSE FOR
A PHOTO.

students, Troy is also the captain of the school's varsity basketball team, so while the film was shooting, Zac needed to spend three hours every day in basketball practice to hone his skills. He says that the cast basketball players had to practice just as a real team would, doing exactly the same drills and being put under the same pressure from their coach − all this while doing the rehearsals and learning the choreography! Zac has talked about how much he enjoyed learning to play basketball really well, and still enjoys a game if he has a chance.

After the first *High School Musical* film came out, Zac told interviewers about how much he enjoyed playing Troy. He thinks that Troy is someone that most teens can identify with in some way. 'He's just growing up. The character is very identifiable with kids growing up all over the world today,' he said at the time. 'Troy seems like every guy to me. That's what I've always liked about him.' An 'everyguy', possibly − but if so, definitely one with an extra dash of cool. Which is probably why Zac once described him as a dream character to play. 'He gets all the cool girls. He's kind of like Danny Zuko in *Grease*. I think that every guy would like to have been more like Troy when they were in high school. I wish I was more like him because he's so cool.' No doubt there are plenty of 'cool girls' who think Zac is pretty perfect as he is…

There's probably another reason that Zac enjoyed the role, too. In the first film, Troy meets Gabriella Montez (Vanessa Hudgens) and romance blossoms – and of course we now know that it was during the filming of the movie that Zac and Vanessa started dating. No wonder they won an award for their chemistry!

He also really enjoyed the way his character developed as more *High School Musical* films were made. 'If Troy gets any cooler, he'll explode,' said Zac, adding that there wasn't much more that he could ask for in his character.

# U is for...

## University

Zac worked really hard when he was at school, and did really well, graduating from high school with a Grade Point Average of 4.3 – basically, straight A's. He did plan on going to university and got a place at the University of Southern California to study film.

'I had friends in the programme and they just raved about it. I was so jealous that they were there,' Zac explains. He decided to apply for a place himself, but his career has got in the way of his plans to study.

'After I was accepted to go, I was deferred for one year and since then, I haven't really had time to go back,' he says. But it seems that with Zac's down to earth attitude to his work, and his determination to keep developing his skills on the job, he's probably learning plenty about film as it is! 'I'm learning so much every day working with great directors. I just worked with Richard Linklater and Burr Steers and also Kenny Ortega. I'm working hand-in-hand with directors and taking home a lot of lessons,' Zac said in 2008. Since then he's signed a producer's deal with a major studio, so it does look as though his ambition to get behind the camera might come to fruition, even without a stint at university.

# V is for...

## Vanessa Hudgens

Zac and his long-term girlfriend Vanessa met on the set of *High School Musical*, of course, but for a while they kept the fact that their off-screen relationship was mirroring their on-screen one pretty quiet. Even people working with them on the second movie didn't twig that they were dating! Despite the undoubted chemistry between them on the *High School Musical* movies, it was a good while before they went public with the fact they were dating, and

Zac's long-term girlfriend Vanessa.

even once that had happened, they were both wary of talking too much about it in public. 'I don't want to be the 19-year-old kid who talks about his relationship in interviews,' Zac said at the time – and he's more or less kept to that ever since. 'It's just not something that you seek attention for, it's never been about that. I feel like I've been fighting that from day one,' he says. 'It's one thing to be recognised for your work but to be recognised for your personal life, it's not admirable, I've never been interested in that.'

But despite their reluctance to talk about their relationship, it is very clear that the attraction between them was pretty much immediate. 'The first time I met Vanessa, I was blown away with her beauty and her charm and elegance,' says Zac, who is clearly smitten. 'They were effortless. I noticed that at the very first audition when we paired up together and we hadn't known each other at all.' Vanessa agrees. 'Right off the bat, we had a connection. I think everybody could see it,' she said. 'And he was adorable. I mean, he wasn't the guy that he is today. Like, he had a gap in his teeth. He was a whole different person.'

As well as loving her personality, Zac is also very admiring of Vanessa's talent as an actress. He said: 'The first time I saw the movie, it jumped out to me how much Vanessa could really light up the screen. She is a brilliant performer. She's such a kind, caring individual and that just really shows through the character. Vanessa is incredible, she really stands above the rest of the competition and I admire her for that.' Zac has also said that he'd love the opportunity to make another film with Vanessa, describing her as his 'best friend' as well as his girlfriend and an actress he admires. Zac says that he has not met anyone who compares with Vanessa, because 'she simply outshines all other girls because of her strong personality.' Awww!

There are continual rumours in the press about Zac and Vanessa (or 'Zanessa' as they are often called by fans). If they're not breaking up, or one or both of them isn't secretly dating someone else, they're moving in together, getting engaged or having a baby. But the couple keep it low-key; with both Zac and Vanessa saying that marriage isn't on either of their to do lists for a while. It seems that they're happy enough as they are, and hopefully they'll stay that way.

Vanessa attributes the success of their relationship to the fact that she's pretty relaxed and doesn't get jealous or possessive. 'Trust is everything,' she says. 'I think it's important not to be a jealous girlfriend because I think it's something that a lot of girls do, and it can be unattractive.'

# Video Games

Zac is a fan of video games – he has said in the past that if he wasn't an actor, his dream job would be designing and testing games – and when he received his first pay cheque from *High School Musical*, he went out and bought 'a lot of video game systems.' He took part in the launch events for the *Halo 3* Xbox game back in 2007, and talked about how much he enjoyed playing games with Matthew Perry when they were making *17 Again* – although he had to admit that Matthew was better at some of the more involved games than he was. He's not got much time for the argument that video game culture causes violence, and dismisses it as nonsense. Well, actually, he uses a word that's a bit ruder than 'nonsense'… 'The last thing I would ever do is hurt another person,' he says, frankly, 'and online I probably kill 200 guys a day.' Zac says that when it comes to video games, he favours a methodical approach – one shot, one kill – because you save bullets that way. Who knew he could sound so bloodthirsty?

More recently, if some sources are to be believed, his fondness for gaming has been causing trouble in

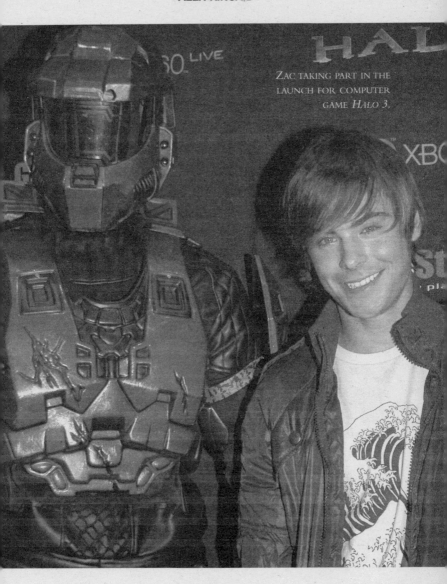

Zac taking part in the launch for computer game *Halo 3*.

his personal life. Earlier this year, there were rumours that Zac was spending so much time on the games console that Vanessa had threatened to dump him if he didn't stop playing. We're told (by an unnamed source) that at first Vanessa tried playing the games too, but she's getting tired of it and is on the verge of telling him: 'It's either me or the Xbox.' We can only speculate as to how accurate this is, but if it is true, Vanessa might take comfort from the fact that she isn't the only girl in the world who has to compete with a games console for her boyfriend's attention!

# Voting

Zac is as private over his politics as he is over most other aspects of his life, but he does do what he can to get other young people involved in voting. He is a registered voter and although, unlike many other stars, he didn't endorse a candidate at the last US Presidential election, he did his best to get people involved, and joined a campaign called 'Declare Yourself'. This was a non–partisan, not-for-profit campaign which encouraged every eligible 18 to 29-year-old in America to register and vote in local and national elections. He appeared in an ad for the campaign in which he talked about how important it was to vote and how the whole nation needed to be involved. 'We're picking officials to represent ourselves,' he said, 'so the more opinions we can have represented, the better.'

# W is for...

## Wealth

Zac works hard, is determined to do well, and is clearly successful. In 2008, *Forbes* magazine reported that he had earned $5.8 million in the previous 12 months! But our favourite actor does his best to keep his feet on the ground and not let success, or wealth, change him. His friends say that it's always been obvious that he isn't in show business for the money, and he's not driven by making a heap of cash – which is why he turns

Zac is escorted from his car by security guards.

down potentially well paid jobs if they're not what he really wants to do.

He describes his house as small and modest, he doesn't have a garage full of cars, and he tries to live well within his income. 'I've always, always lived below my means,' he told the *Sydney Morning Herald*. 'I would not consider myself a big spender; I buy what I need and that's about it. I've never been extravagant, that's not the way I was raised. It's just not who I am.' He has talked about his strict upbringing and how it still affects him – it looks like his parents also taught him to be careful with money. Perhaps his careful attitude also comes from caution about his career. Zac is aware that there are plenty of actors who don't manage to stay in the limelight. 'There's only a handful of people that have long careers. You have to put in the work, you can never be satisfied, never take it for granted,' he says. It sounds like Zac's not wanting to flash the cash is part of a wider determination not to take anything for granted.

# Working out

Zac admits to being a bit of a fitness freak, and says he doesn't feel right unless he starts the day with a morning jog. Some of his fans will no doubt be interested to know that when weather permits, he takes his run without wearing a shirt... He also works out at the gym for an hour, five times a week. That must certainly be at least part of the reason why he was hailed by *People* magazine as having the best body in Hollywood!

# X is for...

## X-rated?

There was a bit of a stir when, in 2008, pictures appeared on the internet which showed Zac and Vanessa with a fan. Fan pictures are common enough, so what was the problem here? Well, the pictures in question appeared to have been taken in an adult shop. Was it what it looked like? What could have been going on?

According to Zac, no, it was not at all what it looked like. He was taken aback by the commotion because the pictures were two years old and he and Vanessa had practically forgotten about them. 'It was Hallowe'en Eve, it was just a costume store, and in the back they have an adult section for adult costumes,' he told *Elle* magazine. 'And this nice older woman asked for a photo.' Perhaps Zac and Vanessa should have looked behind them at the shelves before they said yes?

When the pictures came out, as well as the online commotion, Zac found that he had some explaining to do. To his mother. 'I was like, "Mom, calm down, it's not a sex shop." She wouldn't have any of it. My stocking was full of condoms this Christmas.' Zac was lucky – not all mums would have been so understanding if their sons were caught in such a compromising situation, or have such a sense of humour!

# Y is for...

## Years ahead?

Zac is often asked about his plans for the future, and where he wants to be in 10 or 15 years, and it sounds as though he's trying not to make too many plans. He says that he's never been 'the guy with the plan' and that he doesn't know where he wants to end up in 10 years – and he actually doesn't want to know. 'I know that I want to stay current, competitive, make great movies, and strive for innovation,' he says, but he's laid back about what that might mean in terms of a career

path. Zac knows that he's at the beginning of his career and the next few choices he makes could be crucial to where his path ends up taking him, but he's happy to keep his options open. 'I'm pretty sure I could be a million places,' he says.

He claims that he isn't strategic about choosing roles. 'I've never really had any strategy at all. I don't really work that way. I know that when I see a role and it speaks to me, I'm drawn to it and I have to go in that direction,' he says. But is it easy to be so relaxed about your future? Zac admits that learning to relax is a challenge in itself – 'letting things happen naturally, throwing everything against the wall and seeing what sticks,' as he puts it. He has said that he would like to have a go at directing at some point in the future, and it's rumoured that he's about to have a production credit on one of his upcoming projects, but at the moment, Zac says that his only real plan is 'to make good movies for the rest of my life.' And who can argue with that?

# Z is for...

## Zac Efron's Pool Party

*Funny or Die* is a comedy video website founded by Will Ferrell and Adam McKay's production company. It features original and user-generated content. *Funny or Die* is unique in that it contains a good deal of exclusive material from a number of famous contributors and has its own Funny or Die Team which creates original material for the site. Videos are voted on by users of the site; those that are deemed funny stay, but those that are not 'die' and are relegated to the site's 'crypt'.

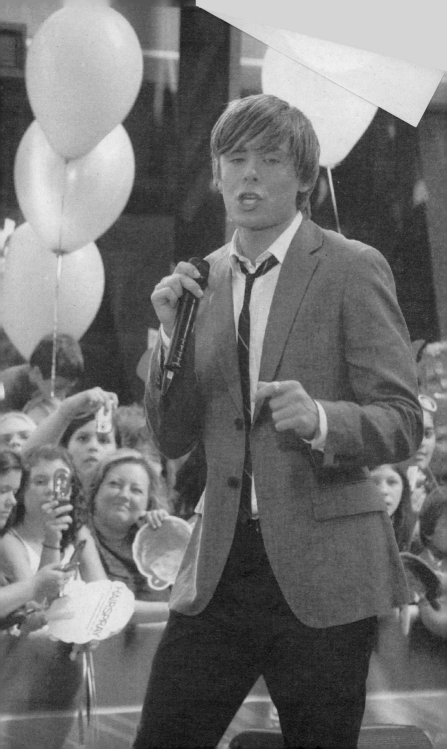

Zac took part in a short comedy film for the site, entitled *Zac Efron's Pool Party*. He appears with fellow teen idols Nicole Richie, Vanessa Hudgens, Justin Long and Lance Bass, along with Queen Latifah and Carmen Electra. The premise of the short film is that Zac is holding a pool party for his friends, where they can hang out, discuss the serious issues of the day (such as philosophy and economics) and have a good time. But the party is crashed by Zac's horrendous 'Uncle Hank' (played by Thomas Lennon) and Hank's equally vile girlfriend Randi (Nicole Sullivan), who are hideously embarrassing and manage to offend practically everyone, humiliating Zac into the bargain.

Highlights of the film include Lance Bass proudly revealing that he hasn't Googled himself for a week, and Zac's mortified reaction when Hank boasts that he was once a guitar tech for the Spin Doctors. Director Adam Shankman said that the project was 'all on the fly and really fun,' and that the cast and crew had a great time making it.

What inspired Adam Shankman to make a video for *Funny or Die*? 'The media forces us to take our lives so seriously but we know we're not curing cancer so we might as well make people laugh, we're entertainers,' he explains. 'It's cool because everyone knows we're not getting paid, so there are no egos.' He said that Vanessa and Zac were really nice and down to earth – and that when the filming was all over, Vanessa was taking the rubbish out and Zac was busy doing the dishes! 'They have no entitlement issues, it's all for one and one for all. Nothing is taken for granted,' he said.

The video went down well and rapidly turned viral, with more than 193,000 people viewing it by the early afternoon of its release, and there have been nearly 2 million views to date. It has attained the status of 'Chosen One' on the site, which means that it's been deemed safe from the 'crypt' and will stay on the website for good. Which means that even more people will be able to watch Zac's 'uncle' telling him, 'Ooh, you smell like waffles!'

# Zefron.com

There are lots of fan sites on the web which are dedicated to our favourite actor – and that is hardly surprising! Zac doesn't have an 'official' fan site, but he does have his favourite. It's called *Charismatic*, or www.zefron.com and it's run by a lady called Kathryn

Vincent. She started the site in 2004 after seeing Zac in *Summerland* – yes, she was a fan before the *High School Musical* sensation! This is one of the reasons that Zac especially appreciates her site. Over the years, Kathryn has collected hundreds of pictures, interviews and other Zac information, and she's able to check facts with Zac, who visits the site, so it's a good place to find out what Zac's up to! Zac's management have described it as a 'credible, accurate source for fans' which is something Kathryn is justifiably proud of. She also takes pride in the fact that she only reproduces what she calls 'respectful' photographs – she doesn't want to encourage the paparazzi and others who take invasive photographs of celebrities.

Zac clearly appreciates the work Kathryn has put into the site, telling *M* magazine that 'she's really changed my life.' He said, 'The webpage is great. She seriously knows stuff about my career before I do!' Kathryn was thrilled by the praise and paid tribute to how normal Zac is, and said that she hoped that she'd meet him one day – 'and maybe ask for a hug!' she added.

Katherine was lucky enough to meet Zac, when he flew her out to interview him on the set of his movie *17 Again* – and she made sure that she got her hug. And really, who can blame her?